INTRODUCTION TO CHILD DEVELOPMENT

INTRODUCTION TO CHILD DEVELOPMENT

Maimun Nisha

ISHA BOOKS
DELHI-110033

Introduction to Child Development

Rs. 625

ISBN : 81-8205-373-0

Published in 2006 in India by
Isha Books
D-43, Prithviraj Road,
Adarsh Nagar, Delhi-110033

Laser Typesetting at : Master Computers, Delhi
Printed at : Salasar Imaging System, Delhi

Contents

Preface

Special educational needs for children may help because of a range of needs, in thinking and understanding, physical and sensory difficulty, speech and language difficulty and how they behave with other people.

Schools, parents and other agencies ca help the children to over come further difficulties very suddenly and easily. So this book eradicate their problems to some extent.

This book covers all the courses of study which follows by university in India. This book covers eight chapters, i.e., understanding the child psychology, prenatal development, neonatal development, neonatal development, methods of child development, Developmental principles, child care, childhood diseases, aspects of development, and special needs of disadvantage child, which is an easy, simple, useful, authentic, concise reference that describes the many aspects of child development.

This book is a precious guide for student, counselors, teachers, child specialists, parents and other related service specialists.

Maimun Nisha

1

Introduction to Child Psychology

Meaning

Child development deals with growth and development of characteristics. It is concerned with the discovery, interpreting and productively individual development. It is also concerned with child guidance and counselling of children.

Child-psychology and child development deals with understanding of growth and development patterns and the development of various characteristics in children.

Child development is defined as a branch of knowledge concerned with both the nature of development and regulation of significant structural, functional and behavioural changes occurring in children as they advance in age and maturity. It deals with understanding the development of characteristics of children and the process through which development starts.

Nature: Child development is natural source Psychologist observe, describe, measure and relate phenomena as they occurs naturally in uncontinued situation. Child development based on naturalistic observation. It manipulate emotions attitudes, and value among the children concept of development pre-supposes that there is a continuity in development. This continuity is lawful and is observed between successive stages of an ongoing growth process and that properties of earlier phase contributes to the properties of subsequent phase. These changes are progressive heredity and environment facilities contribute to process to change. There is also reciprocal changes between organism and the environment.

Importance: Importance of child psychology can be illustrated given the point of view of parents, teachers and guidance experts.

Parents: It enables them to keep a record of the growth of the child if they are interested. The parents became able to know that is the critical period in development, about enriched environment, how such facilities created, how the baby will reached, his curiosity etc.

Child psychology enable the parents to know the technical ideas of dealing with childhood emotions and when resultant frustrations in a more healthier way than by spacing on using the Rod only. The apply the motivational and learning principles to bring changes in their children. Parents can guide their children according to childhood interest. They can held them to develop socialisation and cognitive development. Child psychology is useful to parents in the area of language and socialization.

Teacher: Child psychology is useful to teacher in early childhood period. Teacher know the basic needs of children that are to be compiled in school without which the child areas quit school. Child psychology enables teacher to be acquainted with milestones of development. It enables teacher to find out the behaviour problems in school. Teacher uses most observational techniques. Many teacher spoil the child because they do not know the mental state of child. The knowledge of child psychology in meaningful.

Guidance Experts: In our country child guidance has not been developed except is very big cities and that too very rarely psychologically oriented. These are medically designed with child guidance clinic.

Child guidance is necessary. For this purpose through and comprehensive understanding of child development is essential. So, understanding of the child psychology is necessary because it contributes to later development of personality and behaviour.

Scope

(i) Child psychology are so many and varied.

(ii) Child psychology helping the child who suffers from chronic behaviour problems.

(iii) Child psychology becomes useful in guidance of children.

(iv) Child psychology is necessary for child's personality development.

(v) Child psychology is essential for parents for socialization.

Objectives

Child psychologist have accepted the four fold objectives: observation, prediction, guidance, and central of child behaviour and development.

(i) Child psychology helps one to observe the child behaviour.

(ii) Child psychology helps one to predict child behaviour.

(iii) Child psychology helps one to guide child behaviour.

(iv) Child psychology helps one to control child sbehaviour.

Theory of Child Psychology

Child psychology includes on understanding of the child from the time of concept, the principles by which hereditary vacant are transmitted to children, prenatal case of fetus and the mother, attention paid to factors such as maternal neutrition, disease, Xray, drugs, etc., and including the development of ovum, embroy and foetus.

Child psychology concerned with behaviour of neonate. It also include study of intelligence, emotion language proficiency play, creativity and cognitive development of children.

Child psychology encompassed with the prenatal, perinatal, postnatal growth and development, birth hazards, baby care and ailments of childhood.

Developmental Theory and Investigation to Child Psychology

Focuses on the developmental periods of infancy, and childhood to offer illustrations of the advantages of using developmental theory and research to establish targets for research on intervention, assessment and treatment planning, and evaluation of effective strategies for prevention of childhood disorders. The importance in developmental approaches to research is stressed, and hopes for a future of mutual contributions of developmental and clinical psychology are expressed in light of the fact that, after a troubled history of isolation from one another and even active denigration of one another's goals and methods, developmental and clinical psychology are exhibiting joint recognition of the advantages of collaborative research.

The relation between developmental and child psychology has not always been sanguine. In fact, almost 2 decades ago Selman and Yando (1980) characterized it as a "smoldering civil war," in which different assumptions, methodological proclivities, and goals had historically created a widening schism in communication. Further, "basic research" (e.g., laboratory controlled situations in which all children received the same set of experiences) was portrayed by one camp as being somehow more scientific than applied investigations (e.g., in which children's different experiences with memories, pain, or violence might be explored). There were counter charges of an absence of the utility of developmental findings or of contrived behavioural findings that continued the separation. Some researchers even suggested that those scientists who attempted collaborative research between developmental and clinical psychology were risking their opportunities to obtain tenure (Rolf and Reed, 1984). The friction has not entirely been laid to rest. Recently, for example, a prominent and respected developmental researcher referred in an American Psychological Association (APA) flagship journal to "the 'ratmen' marched into the child psychology laboratories... from other areas of psychology" and imposed "trivial and sometimes inappropriate research questions and paradigms from animal studies... which did not take a developmental perspective" (Hetherington, 1998). The era that gave rise to such sentiments is, fortunately, largely behind us. As Hetherington's dedication of a special issue of the American Psychologist to "Developmental Science" can document, clinical and developmental researchers are now actively working toward collaborative methods and values.

Even early on, savvy scientists voiced their hope for conjoined efforts. Sears (1975), for example, characterized joint efforts in these areas as a "tremendous partnership that always seems to exist when pure and applied sciences" attempt to fulfill real social rather than merely intellectual needs. He argued for the social relevance of the field and underlined the necessity for its multidisciplinary nature. He also recognized and expressed concern that differences in methods and various political turf issues might impede the important process of this emerging field. The relationship has improved, as Sears predicted, in recent years, with a number of additional products to document the rapprochement of disciplines with similar aims. Unfortunately, most psychologists may still fail to profit from developmental theory or offer findings and establish forums in a method likely to contribute to the developmental literature. Similarly, many developmentalists do not offer their research in a manner conducive to adoption by researchers, and many adult researchers are not interested in the origins of the pathology. Sroufe and Rutter (1984) made a compelling case for the emergence of developmental psychopathology, a field singularly different from child psychology.

Child Development—As a Series of Stages

Freud and the psychoanalyst **Erik Erikson** proposed a series of stages of development reflecting the attainment of biological objectives. The stages are expressed in terms of functioning as an individual and with others—within the family and the broader social environment (particularly in Erikson's theories). Although criticized as unscientific and relevant primarily to the era and culture in which they were conceived, these theories introduced the importance of thinking developmentally, that is, of considering the ever-changing physical and psychological capacities and tasks faced by people as they age. They emphasized the concept of "maturation" and moving through the stages of life, adapting to changing physical capacities and new psychological and social challenges. And they described mental health problems associated with failure to achieve milestones and objectives in their developmental schemes.

These theories have guided generations of psychodynamic therapists and child development experts. They are important to understand as the underpinnings of many therapeutic approaches, such as interpersonal therapy, some of which have been evaluated and found to be efficacious for some conditions. By and large, however, these theories have rarely been tested empirically.

Normal Stages of Child Development (Birth to 5 Years)

This presents an overview of child development from birth to five years of age. It is important to keep in mind that the time frames presented are averages and some children may achieve various developmental milestones earlier or later than the average but still be within the normal range. This information is presented to help parents understand what to expect from their child. Any questions you may have about your child's development should be shared with his doctor.

Physical and Language	*Emotional*	*Social*
Birth to 1 month		
Feedings: 5-8 per day Sleep: 20 hrs per day Sensory Capacities: Makes basic distinctions in vision, hearing, smelling, tasting, touch, temperature, and perception of pain	Generalized Tension	Helpless Asocial Fed by mother
2 to 3 months		
Sensory Capacities: colour perception, visual exploration, oral exploration. cries, coos, grunts Motor Ability: control of eye muscles, lifts head when on stomach.	Delight Distress Smiles at a Face	Visually fixates at a face, smiles at a face, may be Sounds: soothed by rocking.
4 to 6 months		
Sensory Capacities: localizes sounds Sounds: Babbling, makes most vowels and about half of the consonants Feedings: 3-5 per day. Motor Ability: Control of head and arm movements, purposive grasping, rolls over.	Enjoys being cuddled	Recognizes his mother. Distinguishes between familiar persons and strangers, no longer smiles indiscriminately. Expects feeding, dressing, and bathing.

(Contd.)

(Table Contd.)

Physical and Language	*Emotional*	*Social*
7 to 9 months		
Motor Ability: Control of trunk and hands, sits without support, crawls about.	Specific emotional attachment to mother. Protests separation from mother.	Enjoys "peek-a-boo"
10 to 12 months		
Motor Ability: Control of legs and feet, stands, creeps, opposition of thumb and forefinger. Language: Says one or two words, imitates sounds, responds to simple commands. Feedings: 3 meals, 2 snacks Sleep: 12 hours, 2 naps.	Anger Affection Fear of strangers Curiousity, exploration.	Responsive to own name. Wave bye-bye. Plays pat-a-cake, understands "no-no!" Gives and takes objects.
1 to 1½ years		
Motor Ability: Creeps up stairs, walks (10-20 min), makes lines on paper with crayon.	Dependent Behaviour Very upset when separated from mother Fear of Bath.	Obeys limited commands. Repeats a few words. Interested in his mirror image. Feeds himself.
1½ to 2 years		
Motor Ability: Runs, kicks a ball, builds 6 cube tower (2 yrs) Capable of bowel and bladder control. Language: Vocabulary of more than 200 words Sleep: 12 hours at night, 1-2 hr nap.	Temper tantrums (1-3 yrs) Resentment of new baby.	Does opposite of what he is told (18 months).
2 to 3 years		
Motor Ability: Jumps off a step, rides a tricycle, uses crayons, builds a 9-10 cube tower. Language: Starts to use short sentences controls and explores world with language, stuttering may appear briefly.	Fear of separation Negativistic (2½ yrs) Violent emotions, anger Differentiates facial expressions of anger, sorrow, and joy. Sense of humor (Plays tricks).	Talks, uses "I" "me" "you" Copies parents' actions. Dependent, clinging, possessive about toys, enjoys playing alongside another child. Negativism (2½ yrs). Resists parental demands. Gives orders. Rigid insistence on sameness of routine. Inability to make decisions.

(Contd.)

(Table Contd.)

Physical and Language	*Emotional*	*Social*
3 to 4 years Motor Ability: Stands on one leg, jumps up and down, draws a circle and a cross (4 yrs). Self-sufficient in many routines of home life.	Affectionate toward parents. Pleasure in genital manipulation. Romantic attachment to parent of opposite sex (3 to 5 yrs). Jealousy of same sex parent. Imaginary fears of dark, injury, etc. (3 to 5 years).	Likes to share, uses "we". Cooperative play with other children, nursery school. Imitates parents. Beginning of identification with same sex parent, practices sex-role activities. Intense curiosity and interest in other children's bodies. Imaginary friend.
4 to 5 years Motor Ability: Mature motor control, skips, broad jumps, dresses himself, copies a square and a triangle. Language: Talks clearly, uses adult speech sounds, has mastered basic grammar, relates a story, knows over 2,000 words (5 yrs).	Responsibility and guild. Feels pride in accomplishment.	Prefers to play with other children, becomes competitive prefers sex-appropriate activities.

Erikson's Eight Stages of Development Theory

1. Learning Basic Trust Versus Basic Mistrust (Hope)

Chronologically, this is the period of infancy through the first one or two years of life. The child, well-handled, nurtured, and loved, develops trust and security and a basic optimism. Badly handled, he becomes insecure and mistrustful.

2. Learning Autonomy Versus Shame (Will)

The second psychosocial crisis, Erikson believes, occurs during early childhood, probably between about 18 months or 2 years and 3½ to 4 years of age. The "well-parented" child emerges from this stage sure of himself, elated with his new found control, and proud rather than ashamed. Autonomy is not, however, entirely synonymous with assured self-possession, initiative, and independence but, at least for children in the early part of this psychosocial crisis, includes stormy self-will, tantrums, stubbornness, and negativism. For example, one sees may 2 year olds resolutely folding their arms to prevent their mothers from holding their hands as they cross the street. Also, the sound of "NO" rings through the house or the grocery store.

3. Learning Initiative Versus Guilt (Purpose)

Erikson believes that this third psychosocial crisis occurs during what he calls the "play age," or the later pre-school years (from about 3½ to, in the United States culture, entry into formal school). During it, the healthily developing child learns: (1) to imagine, to broaden his skills through active play of all sorts, including fantasy (2) to cooperate with others (3) to lead as well as to follow. Immobilized by guilt, he is: (1) fearful (2) hangs on the fringes of groups (3) continues to depend unduly on adults and (4) is restricted both in the development of play skills and in imagination.

4. Industry Versus Inferiority (Competence)

Erikson believes that the fourth psychosocial crisis is handled, for better or worse, during what he calls the "school age," presumably up to and possibly including some of junior high school. Here the child learns to master the more formal skills of life: (1) relating with peers according to rules (2) progressing from free play to play that may be elaborately structured by rules and may demand formal teamwork, such as baseball and (3) mastering social studies, reading, arithmetic. Homework is a necessity, and the need for self-discipline increases yearly. The child who, because of his successive and successful resolutions of earlier psychosocial crisis, is trusting, autonomous, and full of initiative will learn easily enough to be industrious. However, the mistrusting child will doubt the future. The shame—and guilt-filled child will experience defeat and inferiority.

5. Learning Identity Versus Identity Diffusion (Fidelity)

During the fifth psychosocial crisis (adolescence, from about 13 or 14 to about 20) the child, now an adolescent, learns how to answer satisfactorily and happily the question of "Who am I?" But even the best-adjusted of adolescents experiences some role identity diffusion: most boys and probably most girls experiment with minor delinquency; rebellion flourishes; self-doubts flood the youngster, and so on.

Erikson believes that during successful early adolescence, mature time perspective is developed; the young person acquires self-certainty as opposed to self-consciousness and self-doubt. He comes to experiment with different-usually constructive—roles rather than adopting a "negative identity" (such as delinquency). He actually anticipates achievement, and achieves, rather than being "paralyzed" by feelings of inferiority or by an inadequate time perspective. In later adolescence, clear sexual identity-manhood or womanhood—is established. The adolescent seeks leadership (someone to inspire him), and gradually develops a set of ideals (socially congruent and desirable, in the case of the successful adolescent). Erikson believes that, in our culture, adolescence affords a "psychosocial moratorium," particularly for middle—and upper-class American children. They do not yet have to "play for keeps," but can experiment, trying various roles, and thus hopefully find the one most suitable for them.

6. Learning Intimacy Versus Isolation (Love)

The successful young adult, for the first time, can experience true intimacy—the sort of intimacy that makes possible good marriage or a genuine and enduring friendship.

7. Learning Generativity Versus Self-Absorption (Care)

In adulthood, the psychosocial crisis demands generativity, both in the sense of marriage and parenthood, and in the sense of working productively and creatively.

8. Integrity Versus Despair (Wisdom)

If the other seven psychosocial crisis have been successfully resolved, the mature adult develops the peak of adjustment; integrity. He trusts, he is independent and dares the new. He works hard, has found a well-defined role in life, and has developed a self-concept with which he is happy. He can be intimate without strain, guilt, regret, or lack of realism; and he is proud of what he creates—his children, his work, or his hobbies. If one or more of the earlier psychosocial crises have not been resolved, he may view himself and his life with disgust and despair.

These eight stages, or the psychosocial crises, are plausible and insightful descriptions of how personality develops but at present they are descriptions only. Helping the child through the various stages and the positive learning that should accompany them is a complex and difficult task, as any worried parent or teacher knows. Search for the best ways of accomplishing this task accounts for much of the research in the field of child development.

Socialization, then is a learning—teaching process that, when successful, results in the human organism's moving from its infant state of helpless but total egocentricity to its ideal adult state of sensible conformity coupled with independent creativity.

Piaget Theory of Intellectual Development in Children

This page presents an overview of the development of intellectual abilities. Children are not little adults. Until they reach the age of 15 or so they are not capable of reasoning as

Piaget's Stages of Cognitive Development

Developmental Stage and Approximate Age	*Characteristic Behaviour*
Sensory Motor Period (0-24 months)	
Reflexive Stage (0-2 months)	Simple reflex activity such as grasping, sucking.
Primary Circular Reactions (2-4 months)	Reflexive behaviours occur in stereotyped repetition such as opening and closing fingers repetitively.
Secondary Circular Reactions (4-8 months)	Repetition of change actions to reproduce interesting consequences such as kicking one's feet to more a mobile suspended over the crib.
Coordination of Secondary Reactions (8-12 months)	Responses become coordinated into more complex sequences. Actions take on an "intentional" character such as the infant reaches behind a screen to obtain a hidden object.
Tertiary Circular Reactions (12-18 months)	Discovery of new ways to produce the same consequence or obtain the same goal such as the infant may pull a pillow toward him in an attempt to get a toy resting on it.

an adult. The following information is based on the work of *Jean Piaget*. He was not a psychologist. He was a developmental biologist who devoted his life to closely observing and recording the intellectual abilities of infants, children and adolescents. The stages of intellectual development formulated by Piaget appear to be related to major developments in brain growth. The human brain is not fully developed until late adolescence or in the case of males sometimes early adulthood. We often expect children to think like adults when they are not yet capable of doing so. It is important that parents know what to expect from their child as they develop and to be sure that the expectations they may have for their child at a given age are realistic.

2

Prenatal Development

The prenatal period can be considered that time of development and growth of a baby prior to birth. During this time the baby is completely dependent upon the mother for its nutritional needs. This is the most important time of an individual's life as far as nutrition is concerned. This time of rapid growth and development of the baby determines whether or not the developmental potential the child has is met, not only as a baby but, for the rest of his or her life.

During the prenatal period, important organs such as the heart, brain, spinal cord and others are forming. Without the proper levels of vitamins, minerals, and trace minerals, these organs will not develop correctly and birth defects can occur. One example of this is a condition, called spinal bifida, in which the spinal cord does not develop completely before birth. This condition is linked to low levels of vitamins B6, B12 and folic acid in the mother during the prenatal period. Many physicians have realized that it is impossible for the mother to meet the vitamin and mineral needs of her baby and herself through her regular diet. Therefore, the physician recommends a prenatal vitamin in an attempt to meet those needs. However, most of the prenatal vitamins that are prescribed fall short in the form and amount of many minerals and vitamins that are needed.

Not only can nutritional deficiencies affect the baby, but they can also have negative effects on the mother as well. During development, the baby is pulling on all the mother's sources of vitamins and minerals in order to meet its own needs. This stress can lead to conditions that range from low energy levels to gestational diabetes, or pregnancy toxemia. By supplementing a high quality, broad spectrum, vitamin, mineral, and trace mineral supplement women may be able to avoid many of the problems associated with the prenatal period and recover smoothly from the pregnancy while nursing the new baby.

The prenatal period is the most important period of time for the physical development of a human being. Many of the problems seen today during the prenatal period can be avoided, both for the mother and the baby. Supplementation is necessary due to the inadequate amounts of mineral and vitamins in our modern food supply. Even by eating a "perfect" diet, which is almost impossible for the average woman to do, several nutrients would not be present in high enough quantities to avoid these problems.

Prenatal Growth

Prenatal development is divided into three trimesters. During the first two months the developing human is referred to as an embryo. The embryo has three layers from which all body organs develop. During the second trimester the developing human is referred to as a fetus. During the third trimester, the individual is a baby which if born prematurely could survive with extra support. Premature births prior to the third trimester are less likely to survive, even with extraordinary medical care in a neonatal intensive care unit.

First Trimester

First Month

Fertilization, descent of ovum from tube to uterus. Early cell division and formation of embryonic disc from which new organism will develop. Early formation of three layers of cells:

(1) the ectoderm, from which sense organs and nervous system will develop.

(2) the mesoderm, from which circulatory, skeletal and muscular systems will develop.

(3) the endoderm, from which digestive and some glandular systems will develop.

Special layer of cells formed in the uterus which will become the placenta and through which nutritive substances will be carried to the new organism and waste products carried away. Special layer of cells forms the amnion or water-sac, which will surround the developing embryo except at umbilical cord. Heart tube forms and begins to pulsate and force blood to circulate through blood vessels in embryonic disc. Nervous system begins to arise, first in form of neural groove. Development of intestinal tract, lungs, liver and kidneys begins. By end of one month, the embryo is about one-fourth inch long, curled into a crescent, with small nubbins on sides of body indicating incipient arms and legs.

Second Month

Embryo increases in size to about 1½ inches. Bones and muscle begin to round out contours of body. Face and neck develop and begin to give features a human appearance. Forehead very prominent, reflecting precocious development of brain in comparison to rest of body. Limb buds elongate. Muscles and cartilage develop. Sex organs begin to form.

Third Month

Beginning of fetal period. Sexual differentiation continues, with male sexual organs showing more rapid development and the female remaining more neutral. Buds for all 20 temporary teeth laid down. Vocal cords appear; digestive system shows activity.

Stomach cells begin to secrete fluid; liver pours bile into intestine. Kidneys begin functioning, with urine gradually seeping into amniotic fluid. Other waste products passed through placenta into mother's blood. Bones and muscles continue development, and by end of third month spontaneous movements of arms, legs, shoulders and fingers are possible.

Second Trimester

Fourth Month

Lower parts of body show relatively accelerated rate, so that head size decreases from one-half to one-fourth of body size. Back straightens, hands and feet are well-formed. Skin appears dark red, owing to coursing of blood showing through thin skin and wrinkles, owing to absence of underlying fat. Finger closure is possible. Reflexes become more active as muscular maturation continues. Fetus begins to stir and so thrust out arms and legs in movements readily perceived by the mother.

Fifth Month

Skin structures begin to attain final form. Sweat and sebaceous glands are formed and function. Skin derivatives also appear—hair, nails on fingers and toes. Bony axis becomes quite straight and much spontaneous activity occurs. Fetus is lean and wrinkled, about one foot long and weighs about one pound.

Sixth Month

Eyelids which have been fused shut since third month, reopen; eyes are completely formed. Taste buds appear on tongue and in mouth and are, in fact, more abundant than in the infant or adult.

Third Trimester

Seventh Month

Organism capable of independent life from this time on. Cerebral hemispheres cover almost the entire brain. Seven-month fetus can emit a variety of specialized responses. Generally is about 15 inches long and weighs about three pounds.

Eighth and Ninth Month

During this time, finishing touches are being put on the various organs and functional capacities. Fat is formed rapidly over the entire body, smoothing out the wrinkled skin and rounding out body contours. Dull red colour of skin fades so that a firth pigmentation of skin is usually very slight in all races. Activity is usually great and he can change his position within the somewhat crowded uterus. Periods of activity will alternate with periods of quiescence. Fetal organs step up their activity. Fetal heart rate becomes quite rapid. Digestive organs continue to expel more waste products, leading to the formation of a fetal stool, called the me conium, which is expelled shortly after birth. Violent uterine contractions begin, though milder ones have been tolerated earlier, and the fetus is eventually expelled from the womb into an independent physiological existence.

Sign and Symptoms of Pregnancy

Mother

You may notice reddish streaks, or stretch marks, on the skin of your abdomen, breasts or thighs due to hormonal changes and actual tension on the skin. You may develop mild to moderate swelling of your legs, ankles, and feet as well as swelling of the veins in your legs (varicose veins) as a result of your uterus pressing on large blood vessels. Enlarged veins in your rectum (hemorrhoids) can also occur.

You are now entering the third trimester and final phase of your pregnancy. By this time, your baby is completely formed, his/her major internal systems are maturing, and "final touches", eyelashes, fingernails, and hair, are in place. You're seeing more changes, as well.

A few weeks ago you could feel the baby moving inside of you, now you can also see this activity. But that's not the only sign your pregnancy is progressing.

You may notice reddish streaks or stretch marks (also call striae) on the skin of your abdomen, breasts, hips, buttocks, or thighs. These are caused by hormonal changes and actual tension on the skin. Striae fade to a silvery white colour after delivery or may not completely disappear.

Your expanding uterus may be creating other discomforts, too, including edema (swelling) of you legs, ankles and feet, varicose veins and hemorrhoids

1. Tender, swollen breasts
2. Fatigue
3. Implantation bleeding
4. Nausea or vomiting
5. Increased sensitivity to odors
6. Food aversions
7. Frequent urination
8. A missed period
9. Your basal body temperature stays high
10. The proof: A positive home pregnancy test

Most likely you won't notice any pregnancy symptoms until about the time you've missed a period, or a week or two later. If you're not keeping record of your menstrual cycle or if it varies widely from one month to the next, you may not be sure when to expect your period. But if you start to experience some of the symptoms below (not all women get them all) and you haven't had a period for a while, you may very well be pregnant. Take a pregnancy kit to identify the pregnancy.

1. Tender, Swollen Breasts

One of the early hallmarks of pregnancy is *sensitive, sore breasts* caused by increasing levels of hormones. The soreness may feel like an exaggerated version of how your breasts feel before your period. Your discomfort should diminish significantly after the first trimester, as your body adjusts to the hormonal changes.

2. Fatigue

Feeling tired all of a sudden? No, make that *exhausted*. Increased levels of the hormone progesterone and the stress your body undergoes as it adapts to pregnancy can make you feel as if you've run a marathon when all you've done is put in a day at work. You should start to feel more energetic once you hit your second trimester, although fatigue usually returns in the third trimester.

3. Implantation Bleeding

Some women have a small amount of vaginal bleeding around 11 or 12 days after conception (close to the time you might notice a missed period). The bleeding may be caused by the fertilized egg burrowing into the blood-rich lining of your uterus—a process that starts just six days after fertilization—but no one knows for sure. The bleeding is very light (appearing as red spotting or pink or reddish-brown staining) and lasts only a day or two. (Let your practitioner know if you notice any bleeding or spotting, particularly if it's accompanied by pain, since this can be a sign of an ectopic pregnancy.)

4. Nausea or Vomiting

If you're like most women, *morning sickness* won't hit you until about a month after conception. (A lucky few escape it altogether.) But some women do start to feel queasy a bit earlier. And not just in the morning, either—pregnancy-related nausea and vomiting can be a problem morning, noon, or night. About half of women with nausea feel complete relief by the beginning of the second trimester. For most of the rest it takes another month or so for the queasiness to ease up.

5. Increased Sensitivity to Odors

It's not uncommon if you're newly pregnant to feel repulsed by the smell of a bologna sandwich or cup of coffee and for certain aromas to trigger your gag reflex. Though no one knows for sure, this may be a side effect of rapidly increasing amounts of estrogen in your system.

6. Food Aversions

While some women insist they crave certain foods during pregnancy, food aversions are even more common. You may suddenly find that certain foods you used to enjoy are now completely repulsive to you. This feeling may come and go or last throughout your pregnancy.

7. Frequent Urination

Shortly after you become pregnant, you may find yourself hurrying to the bathroom all the time. Why? Mostly because during pregnancy the amount of blood and other fluids in your body increases, which leads to extra fluid being processed by your kidneys and ending up in your bladder. This symptom may start as early as six weeks into your first trimester and continue or worsen as your pregnancy progresses and your growing baby exerts more pressure on your bladder.

8. A Missed Period

If you're usually pretty regular and your period doesn't arrive on time, you'll probably take a *pregnancy test* long before you notice any of the above symptoms. But if you're not regular or you're not keeping track of your cycle, nausea and breast tenderness and extra trips to the bathroom may signal pregnancy before you realize you didn't get your period.

9. Your Basal Body Temperature Stays High

If you've been *charting your basal body temperature* and you see that your temperature has stayed elevated for 18 days in a row, you're probably pregnant.

10. The Proof: A Positive Home Pregnancy Test

In spite of what you might read on the box, many *home pregnancy tests* are not sensitive enough to detect pregnancy until about a week after a missed period. So if you decide to take one earlier than that and get a negative result, try again in a few days. Once you've gotten a positive result, make an appointment with your practitioner.

Environmental Factors Influencing Prenatal Development

The age, weight, and height of women affect risk during pregnancy. Girls aged 15 and younger are at increased risk of pre-eclampsia (a type of high blood pressure that develops during pregnancy). Young girls are also at increased risk of having underweight (small-for-gestational-age) or undernourished babies. Women aged 35 and older are at increased risk of problems such as high blood pressure, gestational diabetes (diabetes that develops during pregnancy), and complications during labor.

Women who weigh less than 100 pounds before becoming pregnant are more likely to have small, underweight babies. Obese women are more likely to have very large babies, which may be difficult to deliver. Also, obese women are more likely to develop gestational diabetes and pre-eclampsia.

Women shorter than 5 feet are more likely to have a small pelvis, which may make movement of the fetus through the pelvis and vagina (birth canal) difficult during labor. For example, the fetus's shoulder is more likely to lodge against the pubic bone. This complication is called shoulder dystocia. Also, short women are more likely to have preterm labor and a baby who has not grown as much as expected.

Structural abnormalities in the reproductive organs increase the risk of a miscarriage. Examples are a double uterus or a weak (incompetent) cervix that tends to open (dilate) as the fetus grows.

Drugs

Some drugs taken during pregnancy cause birth defects. Examples are alcohol, some antibiotics, and Angiotensin-Converting Enzyme (ACE) inhibitors (taken during the last two trimesters). Taking drugs that block the actions of folic acid can also cause birth defects (a deficiency of folic acid increases the risk of having a baby with a birth defect). Using cocaine may cause birth defects, premature detachment of the placenta (placental abruption), and premature birth. Smoking cigarettes increases the risk of having a baby with a low birth weight. Early in pregnancy, women are asked if they are using any of these drugs. Of particular concern are alcohol, cocaine, and cigarette smoking.

Problems in a Previous Pregnancy

When women have had a problem in one pregnancy, they are more likely to have a problem, often the same one, in subsequent pregnancies. Such problems include having had a premature baby, an underweight baby, a baby that weighed more than 10 pounds, a baby with birth defects, a previous miscarriage, a late delivery (after 42 weeks of pregnancy), Rh incompatibility that required a blood transfusion to the fetus, or a delivery that required a cesarean section. If women have had a baby who died shortly after birth, they are also more likely to have problems in subsequent pregnancies.

Women may have a condition that tends to make the same problem recur. For example, women with diabetes are more likely to have babies that weigh more than 10 pounds at birth.

Women who had a baby with a genetic disorder or birth defect are more likely to have another baby with a similar problem. Genetic testing of the baby, even if stillborn, and of both parents may be appropriate before another pregnancy is attempted. If these women become pregnant again, tests such as ultrasonography, chronic villus sampling, and amniocentesis may help determine whether the fetus has a genetic disorder or birth defect.

Having had six or more pregnancies increases the risks of very rapid labor and excessive bleeding after delivery. It also increases the risk of a dislocated placenta.

Disorders Present before Pregnancy

Before becoming pregnant, women may have a disorder that can increase the risk of problems during pregnancy. These women should talk with a doctor and try to get in the best physical condition possible before they become pregnant. After they become pregnant, they may need special care, often from an interdisciplinary team. The team may include an obstetrician (who may also be a specialist in the disorder), a specialist in the disorder, and other health care practitioners (such as nutritionists).

Heart Disease: Most women who have heart disease—including heart valve disorders (such as mitral valve prolapse) and some birth defects of the heart—can safely give birth to healthy children, without any permanent ill effects on heart function or life span. However, women who have heart failure before pregnancy are at considerable risk of problems.

Pregnancy requires the heart to work harder. Consequently, pregnancy may worsen heart disease or cause heart disease to produce symptoms for the first time. Usually, serious problems, including death of the woman or fetus, occur only when heart disease is severe before the woman becomes pregnant. About 1% of women who have severe heart disease before becoming pregnant die as a result of the pregnancy, usually because of heart failure.

The risk of problems increases throughout pregnancy as demands on the heart increase. Pregnant women with heart disease may become unusually tired and may need to limit their activities. Rarely, women with severe heart disease are advised to have an abortion early in pregnancy. Risk is also increased during labor and delivery. After delivery, women with severe heart disease may not be out of danger for at least 6 months, depending on the type of heart disease.

Heart disease in pregnant women may affect the fetus. The fetus may be born prematurely. Women with birth defects of the heart are more likely to have children with similar birth defects. Ultrasonography can detect some of these defects before the fetus is born. If severe heart disease in a pregnant woman suddenly worsens, the fetus may die.

During labor, women who have severe heart disease may be given an epidural anesthetic, which blocks sensation in the lower spinal cord and prevents women from pushing. Pushing during labor strains the heart, because it increases the amount of blood returning to the heart. Because pushing is not possible, the baby may have to be delivered with forceps.

For women with some types of heart disease, pregnancy is inadvisable because it so increases their risk of death. Primary pulmonary hypertension and Eisenmenger's syndrome are examples. If women who have one of these disorders become pregnant, doctors advise them to terminate the pregnancy as early as possible.

High Blood Pressure: Women who have high blood pressure (chronic hypertension) before they become pregnant are more likely to have potentially serious problems during pregnancy. These problems include pre-eclampsia (a type of high blood pressure that develops during pregnancy, worsening of high blood pressure, a fetus that does not grow as much as expected, premature detachment of the placenta from the uterus (placental abruption), and stillbirth.

For most women with moderately high blood pressure (140/90 to 150/100 millimeters of mercury [mm Hg]), treatment with antihypertensive drugs is not recommended. Such treatment does not seem to reduce the risk of pre-eclampsia, premature detachment of the placenta, or a stillbirth nor to improve the growth of the fetus. However, some women are treated to prevent pregnancy from causing episodes of even higher blood pressure (which require hospitalization).

For women whose blood pressure is higher than 150/100 mm Hg, treatment with anti-hypertensive drugs is recommended. Treatment can reduce the risk of stroke and other complications due to very high blood pressure. Treatment is also recommended for women who have high blood pressure and a kidney disorder because if high blood pressure is not controlled well, the kidneys may be damaged further.

Most anti-hypertensive drugs used to treat high blood pressure can be used safely during pregnancy. However, Angiotensin-Converting Enzyme (ACE) inhibitors are discontinued during pregnancy, particularly during the last two trimesters. These drugs can cause severe kidney damage in the fetus. As a result, the baby may die shortly after birth.

During pregnancy, women with high blood pressure are monitored closely to make sure blood pressure is well controlled, the kidneys are functioning normally, and the fetus is growing normally. However, premature detachment of the placenta cannot be prevented or anticipated. Often, a baby must be delivered early to prevent stillbirth or complications due to high blood pressure (such as stroke) in the woman.

Anemia: Having a hereditary anemia, such as sickle cell disease, hemoglobin S-C disease, and some thalassemias, increases the risk of problems during pregnancy. Before delivery, blood tests are routinely performed to check for hemoglobin abnormalities in women who are at increased risk of having these abnormalities because of race, ethnic background, or family history. Chorionic villus sampling or amniocentesis may be performed to detect a hemoglobin abnormality in the fetus.

Women who have sickle cell disease are particularly at risk of developing infections during pregnancy. Pneumonia, urinary tract infections, and infections of the uterus are the most common. About one-third of pregnant women who have sickle cell disease develop high blood pressure during pregnancy. A sudden, severe attack of pain, called sickle cell crisis, may occur during pregnancy as at any other time. Heart failure and blockage of arteries of the lungs by blood clots (pulmonary embolism), which may be life threatening, may also occur. Bleeding during labor or after delivery may be more severe. The fetus may grow slowly or not as much as expected. The fetus may even die. The more severe sickle cell disease was before pregnancy, the higher the risk of health problems for pregnant women and the fetus and the higher the risk of death for the fetus during pregnancy. With regular blood transfusions, women are less likely to have sickle cell crises but are more likely to reject the transfused blood. This condition, called alloimmunization, can be life threatening.

Also, transfusions to pregnant women do not reduce risks for the fetus.

Kidney Disorders: Women with a severe kidney disorder before pregnancy are more likely to have problems during pregnancy. Kidney function may rapidly worsen during pregnancy. High blood pressure, which often accompanies a kidney disorder, may also worsen, and pre-eclampsia (a type of high blood pressure that develops during pregnancy) may develop. The fetus may not grow as much as expected or may be stillborn. In pregnant women who have a kidney disorder, kidney function and blood pressure are monitored closely as is the growth of the fetus. Often, the baby must be delivered early.

Women who have had a kidney transplant that has been in place for 2 or more years are usually able to safely give birth to healthy babies if their kidneys are functioning normally, if they have had no episodes of rejection, and if their blood pressure is normal. Many women who have a kidney disorder and who undergo hemodialysis regularly can also give birth to healthy babies.

Seizure Disorders: For most women who take anticonvulsants to treat a seizure disorder, the frequency of seizures does not change during pregnancy. However, sometimes the dose of the anticonvulsant must be increased.

Taking anticonvulsants increases the risk of birth defects. Women who take anticonvulsants should discuss the risk of birth defects with an expert in the field, preferably before they become pregnant. Some women may be able to safely discontinue anticonvulsants during pregnancy, but most women should continue to take the drugs. The risks resulting from not taking the drugs (resulting in more frequent seizures, which can harm the fetus and the woman) usually outweigh the risks resulting from taking them during pregnancy.

Sexually Transmitted Diseases: Women who have a sexually transmitted disease may have problems during pregnancy. Chlamydia infection may cause preterm labor and premature rupture of the membranes containing the fetus. It can also cause conjunctivitis in newborns, as can gonorrhea. Syphilis in pregnant women may be transmitted to the fetus through the placenta. Syphilis can cause several birth defects.

About one fourth of pregnant women who have untreated Human Immunodeficiency Virus (HIV) infection, which causes AIDS, transmit it to their baby. Experts recommend that women with HIV infection take antiretroviral drugs during pregnancy. When pregnant women take these drugs, the risk of transmitting HIV to their baby is reduced to less than 2%. For some women with HIV infection, delivery by cesarean section, planned in advance, may further reduce the risk of transmitting HIV to the baby. Pregnancy does not seem to accelerate the progress of HIV infection in women.

Genital herpes can be transmitted to a baby during a vaginal delivery. A baby who is infected with herpes can develop a life-threatening brain infection called herpes encephalitis. If herpes produces sores in the genital area late in pregnancy, women are usually advised to give birth by cesarean section, so that the virus is not transmitted to the baby. If no sores are present, the risk of transmission is very low.

Diabetes: For women who have diabetes before they become pregnant, the risks of complications during pregnancy depend on how long diabetes has been present and whether complications of diabetes, such as high blood pressure and kidney damage, are present. In some women, diabetes develops during pregnancy; this disorder is called gestational diabetes The risk of complications during pregnancy can be reduced by controlling the level of sugar (glucose) in the blood.

The level should be kept as nearly normal as possible throughout pregnancy. Measures to control the blood sugar level should be started before pregnancy. Most pregnant women are asked to measure their blood sugar level several times a day at home. Controlling diabetes is particularly important late in pregnancy. Then, the blood sugar level tends to increase because the body becomes less responsive to insulin. A higher dose of insulin is usually needed.

If diabetes is poorly controlled very early in the pregnancy, the risks of early miscarriage and significant birth defects are increased. When diabetes is poorly controlled later in pregnancy, the fetus is large and the risk of stillbirth is increased. A large fetus is less likely to pass easily through the vagina and is more likely to be injured during vaginal delivery. Consequently, delivery by cesarean section is often necessary. The risk of pre-eclampsia (a type of high blood pressure that occurs during pregnancy) is also increased for women with diabetes.

The fetus's lungs tend to mature slowly. If an early delivery is being considered (for example, because the fetus is large), the doctor may remove and analyze a sample of the fluid that surrounds the fetus (amniotic fluid). This procedure, called amniocentesis, helps the doctor determine whether the fetus's lungs are mature enough for the newborn to breathe air.

Newborns of women with diabetes are at increased risk of having low sugar, low calcium, and high bilirubin levels in the blood. Hospital staff members measure the levels of these substances and observe the newborns for symptoms of these abnormalities.

For women with diabetes, the requirement for insulin drops dramatically needed immediately after delivery. But the requirement usually returns to what it was before pregnancy within about one week.

Liver and Gallbladder Disorders: Women who have chronic viral hepatitis or cirrhosis (scarring of the liver) are more likely to miscarry or to give birth prematurely. Cirrhosis can cause varicose veins to develop around the esophagus. Pregnancy slightly increases the risk of massive bleeding from these veins, especially during the last three months of pregnancy.

Pregnant women who develop gallstones are closely monitored. If a gallstone blocks the gallbladder or causes an infection, surgery may be necessary. This surgery is usually safe for pregnant women and the fetus.

Asthma: In about half of the women who have asthma and become pregnant, the frequency or severity of asthma attacks does not change during pregnancy. About one fourth of the women improve during pregnancy, and about one-fourth get worse. If pregnant women with severe asthma are treated with prednisone some, the risk that the fetus will not grow as much as expected or will be born prematurely is increased.

Because asthma can change during pregnancy, doctors may ask women with asthma to use a peak flow meter to monitor their breathing more often. Pregnant women with asthma should see their doctor regularly so that treatment can be adjusted as needed. Maintaining good control of asthma is important. Inadequate treatment can result in serious problems, can be taken during pregnancy. Inhalation is the preferred way for taking these drugs. When inhaled, the drugs affect mainly the lungs and affect the whole body and the fetus less. Aminophylline (taken by mouth or given intravenously) and theophylline (taken by mouth) are occasionally used during pregnancy. Corticosteroids are taken by mouth only when other treatments are ineffective. Being vaccinated against the influenza virus during the influenza (flu) season is particularly important for pregnant women with asthma.

Autoimmune Disorders: The abnormal antibodies produced in autoimmune disorders can cross the placenta and cause problems in the fetus. Pregnancy affects different autoimmune disorders in different ways.

Systemic lupus erythematosus (lupus) may appear for the first time, worsen, or become less severe during pregnancy. How a pregnancy affects the course of lupus cannot be predicted, but the most common time for flare-ups is immediately after delivery.

Women who develop lupus often have a history of repeated miscarriages, fetuses that do not grow as much as expected, and preterm delivery. If women have complications due to lupus (such as kidney damage or high blood pressure), the risk of death for the fetus or newborn is increased.

In pregnant women, lupus antibodies may cross the placenta to the fetus. As a result, the fetus may have a very slow heart rate, anemia, a low platelet count, or a low white blood cell count. However, these antibodies gradually disappear over several weeks after the baby is born, and the problems they cause resolve except for the slow heart rate.

In Graves' disease, antibodies stimulate the thyroid gland to produce excess thyroid hormone. These antibodies can cross the placenta and stimulate the thyroid gland in the fetus. As a result, the fetus may have a rapid heart rate and may not grow as much as expected. The fetus's thyroid gland may enlarge, forming a goiter. Very rarely, a goiter may be so, large that it interferes with delivery through the vagina.

Usually, women with Graves' disease take the lowest possible effective dose of propylthiouracil, which slows the activity of the thyroid gland. Physical examinations and measurements of thyroid hormone levels are performed regularly because propylthiouracil crosses the placenta and may prevent the fetus from producing enough thyroid hormone. Often, Graves' disease becomes less severe during the 3rd trimester, so the dose of propylthiouracil can be reduced or stopped. If necessary, the thyroid gland of pregnant women may be removed during the 2nd trimester. These women must begin taking thyroid hormone 24 hours after surgery. Taking this hormone causes no problems for the fetus.

Myasthenia gravis, which causes muscle weakness, does not usually cause serious or permanent complications during pregnancy. However, very rarely during labor, women who have myasthenia gravis may need help with breathing (assisted ventilation). The antibodies that cause this disorder can cross the placenta. So about one of five babies born to women with myasthenia gravis is born with the disorder. However, the resulting muscle weakness in the baby is usually temporary, because the antibodies from the mother gradually disappear and the baby does not produce antibodies of this type.

Idiopathic thrombocytopenic purpura can cause bleeding problems in pregnant women and their babies. If not treated during pregnancy, the disorder tends to become more severe. Corticosteroids, usually prednisone given by mouth, can increase the platelet count and improve blood clotting in pregnant women with this disorder. However, prednisone increases the risk that the fetus will not grow as much as expected or will be born prematurely. High doses of gamma globulin may be given intravenously shortly before delivery. This treatment temporarily increases the platelet count and improves blood clotting. As a result, labor can proceed safely, and women can have a vaginal delivery without uncontrolled bleeding. Pregnant women are given platelet transfusions only when delivery by a cesarean section is needed or when the platelet count is so low that severe bleeding may occur. Rarely, when the platelet count remains dangerously low despite treatment, the spleen, which normally traps and destroys old blood cells and platelets, is removed. The best time for this surgery is during the 2nd trimester.

The antibodies that cause the disorder may cross the placenta to the fetus, resulting rarely in a dangerously low platelet count before and immediately after birth. The baby may then bleed during labor and delivery and may, as a result, be injured or die, especially if bleeding occurs in the brain. The antibodies disappear within several weeks, and the baby's blood then clots normally.

Rheumatoid arthritis does not affect the fetus, but delivery may be difficult for women if arthritis has damaged their hip joints or lower (lumbar) spine. The symptoms of rheumatoid arthritis may lessen during pregnancy, but they usually return to their original level after pregnancy.

Fibroids: Fibroids in the uterus, which are relatively common no cancerous tumors, may increase the risk of preterm labor, abnormal presentation of the fetus, a dislocated placenta, and repeated miscarriages. Rarely, fibroids interfere with the movement of the fetus through the vagina during labor.

Cancer: Because cancer tends to be life threatening and because delays in treatment may reduce the likelihood of successful treatment, cancer is usually treated the same way whether women are pregnant or not. Some of the usual treatments (surgery, chemotherapy drugs, and radiation therapy) may harm the fetus. Thus, some women may consider abortion. However, treatments can sometimes be timed so that risk to the fetus is reduced.

Disorders that Develop during Pregnancy

During pregnancy, women may develop disorders that are not directly related to pregnancy. Some disorders increase the risk of problems for pregnant women or the fetus. They include disorders that cause a high fever, infections, and disorders that require abdominal surgery. Certain disorders are more likely to occur during pregnancy because of the many changes pregnancy causes in a woman's body. Examples are thromboembolic disease, anemia, and urinary tract infections.

Fevers: A disorder that causes a temperature greater than 103°F (39.5°C) during the 1st trimester increases the risk of a miscarriage and defects of the brain or spinal cord in the baby. Fever late in pregnancy increases the risk of preterm labor.

Infections: Some infections that occur coincidentally during a pregnancy can cause birth defects. German measles (rubella) can cause birth defects, particularly of the heart and inner ear. Cytomegalovirus infection can cross the placenta and damage the fetus's liver and brain. Other viral infections that may harm the fetus or cause birth defects include herpes simplex and chickenpox (varicella). Toxoplasmosis, a protozoal infection, may cause miscarriage, death of the fetus, and serious birth defects. Listeriosis, a bacterial infection, can also harm the fetus. Bacterial infections of the vagina (such as bacterial vaginosis) during pregnancy may lead to preterm labor or premature rupture of the membranes containing the fetus. Treatment of infections with antibiotics may reduce the likelihood of these problems.

Disorders that Require Surgery: During pregnancy, a disorder that requires emergency surgery involving the abdomen may develop. This type of surgery increases the risk of preterm labor and can cause a miscarriage, especially early in pregnancy. Thus, surgery is usually delayed as long as possible unless the woman's long-term health may be affected.

If appendicitis develops during pregnancy, surgery to remove the appendix (appendectomy) is performed immediately because a ruptured appendix may be fatal. An appendectomy is not likely to harm the fetus or cause a miscarriage. However, appendicitis may be difficult to recognize during pregnancy. The cramping pain of appendicitis resembles uterine contractions, which are common during pregnancy. The appendix is pushed higher in the abdomen as the pregnancy progresses, so the location of pain due to appendicitis may not be what is expected.

If an ovarian cyst persists during pregnancy, surgery is usually postponed until after the 12th week of pregnancy. The cyst may be producing hormones that are supporting the pregnancy and often disappears without treatment. However, if a cyst or another mass is enlarging, surgery may be necessary before the 12th week. Such a mass may be cancerous.

Obstruction of the intestine during pregnancy can be very serious. If obstruction leads to gangrene of the intestine and peritonitis (inflammation of the membrane that lines the abdominal cavity), a woman may miscarry and her life is endangered. Exploratory surgery is usually performed promptly when pregnant women have symptoms of intestinal obstruction, particularly if they have had abdominal surgery or an abdominal infection.

Thromboembolic Disease: In the United States, thromboembolic disease is the leading cause of death in pregnant women. In thromboembolic disease, blood clots form in blood vessels. They may travel through the bloodstream and block an artery. The risk of developing thromboembolic disease is increased for about 6 to 8 weeks after delivery. Most complications due to blood clots result from injuries that occur during delivery. The risk is much greater after a cesarean section than after vaginal delivery.

Blood clots usually form in the superficial veins of the legs as thrombophlebitis or in the deep veins as deep vein thrombosis. Symptoms include swelling, pain in the calves, and tenderness. The severity of the symptoms does not correlate with the severity of the disease. A clot can move from the legs to the lungs, where it may block one or more arteries in the lungs. This blockage, called pulmonary embolism, can be life threatening. If a clot blocks an artery supplying the brain, a stroke can result. Blood clots can also develop in the pelvis.

Women who have had a blood clot during a previous pregnancy may be given heparin (an anticoagulant) during subsequent pregnancies to prevent blood clots from forming. If women have symptoms suggesting a blood clot, Doppler ultrasonography may be performed to check for clots. If a blood clot is detected, heparin is started without delay. Heparin may be injected into a vein (intravenously) or under the skin (sub-cutaneously). Heparin does not cross the placenta and cannot harm the fetus. Treatment is continued for 6 to 8 weeks after delivery, when the risk of blood clots is high. After delivery, warfarin may be used instead of heparin. Warfarin can be taken by mouth, has a lower risk of complications than heparin, and can be taken by women who are breastfeeding.

If pulmonary embolism is suspected, a lung ventilation and perfusion scan may be performed to confirm the diagnosis. This procedure involves injecting a tiny amount of a radioactive substance into a vein. The procedure is safe during pregnancy because the dose of the radioactive substance is so small. If the diagnosis of pulmonary embolism is still uncertain, pulmonary angiography is required.

Anemia: Most pregnant women develop some degree of anemia because they have an iron deficiency. The need for iron doubles during pregnancy, because iron is needed to make red blood cells in the fetus. Anemia may also develop during pregnancy because of a folic acid deficiency. Anemia can usually be prevented or treated by taking iron and folic acid supplements during pregnancy. However, if anemia becomes severe and persists, the blood's capacity to carry oxygen is decreased. As a result, the fetus may not receive enough oxygen, which is needed for normal growth and development, especially of the brain. Pregnant women who have severe anemia may become excessively tired, short of breath, and light-headed. The risk of preterm labor is increased. A normal amount of bleeding during labor and delivery can cause the anemia in these women to become dangerously severe. Women with anemia are more likely to develop infections after delivery. Also, if folic acid is deficient, the risk of having a baby with a birth defect of the brain or spinal cord, such as spina bifida, is increased.

Urinary Tract Infections: Urinary tract infections are common during pregnancy, probably because the enlarging uterus slows the flow of urine by pressing against the tubes that connect the kidneys to the bladder (ureters). When urine flow is slow, bacteria may not be flushed out of the urinary tract, increasing the risk of an infection. These infections increase the risk of preterm labour and premature rupture of the membranes containing the fetus. Sometimes an infection in the bladder or ureters spreads up the urinary tract and reaches a kidney, causing an infection there. Treatment consists of antibiotic therapy.

Pregnancy Complications

Pregnancy complications are problems that occur only during pregnancy. They may affect the woman, the fetus, or both and may occur at different times during the pregnancy. For example, complications such as a dislocated placenta (placenta previa) or premature detachment of the placenta from the uterus (placental abruption) can cause bleeding from the vagina during the last 3 months of pregnancy. Women who bleed at this time are at risk of losing the baby or of bleeding excessively (hemorrhaging) or dying during labor and delivery. However, most pregnancy complications can be effectively treated.

Ectopic Pregnancy: A Dislocated Pregnancy

Normally, an egg is fertilized in the fallopian tube and becomes implanted in the uterus. However, if the tube is narrowed or blocked, the egg may move slowly or become stuck. The fertilized egg may never reach the uterus, resulting in an ectopic pregnancy. Ectopic pregnancies usually develop in one of the fallopian tubes (as a tubal pregnancy) but may develop in other locations. A fetus in an ectopic pregnancy cannot survive.

One of 100 to 200 pregnancies is an ectopic pregnancy. Risk factors for an ectopic pregnancy include having had a disorder of the fallopian tubes, pelvic inflammatory disease, a previous ectopic pregnancy, exposure to diethylstilbestrol as a fetus, or a tubal ligation (a sterilization procedure) that was unsuccessful or has been surgically reversed.

Symptoms include unexpected vaginal bleeding and cramping. The fetus may grow enough to rupture the structure containing it. If the fallopian tube ruptures (typically after about 6 to 8 weeks), a woman usually feels severe pain in the lower abdomen and may faint. If the tube ruptures later (after about 12 to 16 weeks), the risk of death for the woman is increased, because the fetus and placenta are larger and more blood is lost.

If a woman is unsure she is pregnant, a pregnancy test is performed. If she is pregnant, ultrasonography is performed to determine the location of the fetus. If the uterus is empty, doctors may suspect an ectopic pregnancy. If ultrasonography shows the fetus in a location other than the uterus, the diagnosis is confirmed. Doctors may use a viewing tube called a laparoscope, inserted through a small incision just below the navel, to view the ectopic pregnancy.

Normally, an egg is fertilized in the fallopian tube and becomes implanted in the uterus. However, if the tube is narrowed or blocked, the egg may move slowly or become stuck. The fertilized egg may never reach the uterus, resulting in an ectopic pregnancy. Ectopic pregnancies usually develop in one of the fallopian tubes (as a tubal pregnancy) but may develop in other locations. A fetus in an ectopic pregnancy cannot survive.

One of 100 to 200 pregnancies is an ectopic pregnancy. Risk factors for an ectopic pregnancy include having had a disorder of the fallopian tubes, pelvic inflammatory disease, a previous ectopic pregnancy, exposure to diethylstilbestrol as a fetus, or a tubal ligation (a sterilization procedure) that was unsuccessful or has been surgically reversed.

Symptoms include unexpected vaginal bleeding and cramping. The fetus may grow enough to rupture the structure containing it. If the fallopian tube ruptures (typically after about 6 to 8 weeks), a woman usually feels severe pain in the lower abdomen and may faint. If the tube ruptures later (after about 12 to 16 weeks), the risk of death for the woman is increased, because the fetus and placenta are larger and more blood is lost.

If a woman is unsure she is pregnant, a pregnancy test is performed. If she is pregnant, ultrasonography is performed to determine the location of the fetus. If the uterus is empty, doctors may suspect an ectopic pregnancy. If ultrasonography shows the fetus in a location other than the uterus, the diagnosis is confirmed. Doctors may use a viewing tube called a laparoscope, inserted through a small incision just below the navel, to view the ectopic pregnancy directly.

An ectopic pregnancy must be ended as soon as possible to save the life of the woman. In most women, the fetus and placenta in an ectopic pregnancy must be removed surgically, usually with a laparoscope but sometimes through an incision in the abdomen (in a procedure called laparotomy). Rarely, the uterus is so damaged that a hysterectomy is required. Sometimes, the drug methotrexate, usually given in a single injection, can be used instead of surgery. The drug causes the ectopic pregnancy to shrink and disappear. Occasionally, surgery is needed in addition to methotrexate.

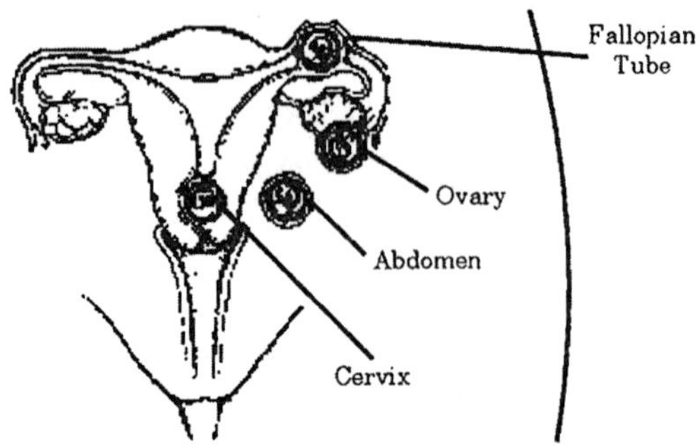

Some problems that result from hormonal changes during pregnancy cause only minor, transient symptoms in pregnant women. For example, the normal hormonal effects of pregnancy can slow the movement of bile through the bile ducts. Cholestasis of pregnancy may result. The most obvious symptom is itching all over the body (usually in the last few months of pregnancy). No rash develops. If itching is intense, cholestyramine may be given. The disorder usually resolves after delivery but tends to recur in subsequent pregnancies.

Hyper Emesis Gravid Arum: Hyper emesis gravid arum is extremely severe nausea and excessive vomiting during pregnancy. Hyper emesis gravid arum differs from ordinary morning sickness. If women vomit often and have nausea to such an extent that they lose weight and become dehydrated, they have hyper emesis gravid arum. If women vomit occasionally but gain weight and are not dehydrated, they do not have hyper emesis gravid arum. The cause of hyper emesis gravid arum is unknown.

Because hyper emesis gravid arum can be life threatening to pregnant women and the fetus, women who have it are hospitalized. An intravenous line is inserted into a vein to give fluids, sugar (glucose), electrolytes, and occasionally vitamins. Women who have this complication are not allowed to eat or drink anything for at least 24 hours. Sedatives, antiemetics, and other drugs are given as needed. After women are rehydrated and vomiting has subsided, they can begin eating frequent, small portions of bland foods. The size of the portions is increased if they can tolerate more food. Usually, vomiting stops within a few days. If symptoms recur, the treatment is repeated. Rarely, if weight loss continues and symptoms persist despite treatment, women are fed via a tube passed through the nose and down the throat to the small intestine for as long as necessary.

Preeclampsia: About 5 per cent of pregnant women develop preeclampsia (toxemia of pregnancy). In this complication, an increase in blood pressure is accompanied by protein in the urine (proteinuria). Preeclampsia usually develops between the 20th week of pregnancy and the end of the first week after delivery. The cause of preeclampsia is unknown. But it is more common among women who are pregnant for the first time, who are carrying two or more fetuses, who have had preeclampsia in a previous pregnancy, who already have high blood pressure or a blood vessel disorder, or who have sickle cell disease. It is also more common among girls aged 15 and younger and among women aged 35 and older.

A variation of severe preeclampsia, called the HELLP syndrome, occurs in some women. It consists of the following:

- Hemolysis (the breakdown of red blood cells)
- Elevated levels of liver enzymes, indicating liver damage
- Low platelet count, making blood less able to clot and increasing the risk of bleeding during and after labor.

In 1 of 200 women who have preeclampsia, blood pressure becomes high enough to cause seizures; this condition is called eclampsia. One fourth of the cases of eclampsia occur after delivery, usually in the first 2 to 4 days. If not treated promptly, eclampsia may be fatal.

Preeclampsia may lead to premature detachment of the placenta from the uterus (placental abruption). Babies of women who have preeclampsia are 4 or 5 times more likely to have problems soon after birth than babies of women who do not have this complication. Babies may be small because the placenta malfunctions or because they are born prematurely.

If mild preeclampsia develops early in the pregnancy, bed rest at home may be sufficient, but such women should see their doctor frequently. If preeclampsia worsens, women are usually hospitalized. There, they are kept in bed and monitored closely until the fetus is mature enough to be delivered safely. Antihypertensives may be needed. A few hours before delivery, magnesium sulfate may be given intravenously to reduce the risk of seizures. If preeclampsia develops near the due date, labor is usually induced and the baby is delivered.

If preeclampsia is severe, the baby may be delivered by cesarean section, which is the quickest way, unless the cervix is already opened (dilated) enough for a prompt vaginal delivery. A prompt delivery reduces the risk of complications for women and the fetus. If blood pressure is high, drugs to lower blood pressure, such as hydralazine or labetalol, may be given intravenously before delivery is attempted. Treatment of the HELLP syndrome is usually the same as that of severe preeclampsia.

After delivery, women who have had preeclampsia or eclampsia are closely monitored for 2 to 4 days because they are at increased risk of seizures. As their condition gradually improves, they are encouraged to walk. They may remain in the hospital for a few days, depending on the severity of the preeclampsia and its complications. After returning home, these women may need to take drugs to lower blood pressure. Typically, they have a checkup at least every 2 weeks for the first few months after delivery. Their blood pressure may remain high for 6 to 8 weeks. If it remains high longer, the cause may be unrelated to preeclampsia.

Gestational Diabetes: About 1 to 3 per cent of pregnant women develop diabetes during pregnancy. This disorder is called gestational diabetes. Unrecognized and untreated, gestational diabetes can increase the risk of health problems for pregnant women and the fetus and the risk of death for the fetus. Gestational diabetes is more common among obese women and among certain ethnic groups, particularly Native Americans, Pacific Islanders, and women of Mexican, Indian, and Asian descent.

Most women with gestational diabetes develop it because they cannot produce enough insulin as the need for insulin increases late in the pregnancy. More insulin is needed to control the increasing level of sugar (glucose) in the blood. Some women may have had diabetes before becoming pregnant, but it was not recognized until they became pregnant.

Some doctors routinely screen all pregnant women for gestational diabetes. Other doctors screen only women who have risk factors for diabetes, such as obesity and certain ethnic backgrounds. A blood test is used to measure the blood sugar level. Women who have gestational diabetes are usually taught to measure their blood sugar levels with a home blood sugar monitoring device.

Treatment consists of eliminating high-sugar foods from the diet, eating to avoid excess weight gain during the pregnancy, and, if the blood sugar level is high, taking insulin. After delivery, gestational diabetes usually disappears. However, many women who have gestational diabetes develop type 2 diabetes as they become older.

Rh Incompatibility: Rh incompatibility occurs when a pregnant woman has Rh-negative blood and the fetus has Rh-positive blood, inherited from a father who has Rh-positive blood. In about 13% of marriages in the United States, the man has Rh-positive blood and the woman has Rh-negative blood.

The Rh factor is a molecule that occurs on the surface of red blood cells of some people. Blood is Rh-positive if red blood cells have the Rh factor and Rh-negative if they do not. Problems can occur if the fetus's Rh-positive blood enters the woman's bloodstream. The woman's immune system may recognize the fetus's red blood cells as foreign and produce antibodies, called Rh antibodies, to destroy the fetus's red blood cells. The production of these antibodies is called Rh sensitization.

During a first pregnancy, Rh sensitization is unlikely, because no significant amount of the fetus's blood is likely to enter the woman's bloodstream until delivery. So the fetus or newborn rarely has problems. However, once a woman is sensitized, problems are more likely with each subsequent pregnancy in which the fetus's blood is Rh-positive. In each pregnancy, the woman produces Rh antibodies earlier and in larger amounts.

If Rh antibodies cross the placenta to the fetus, they may destroy some of the fetus's red blood cells. If red blood cells are destroyed faster than the fetus can produce new ones, the fetus can develop anemia. Such destruction is called hemolytic disease of the fetus (erythroblastosis fetalis) or of the newborn. In severe cases, the fetus may die.

At the first visit to a doctor during a pregnancy, women are screened to determine whether they have Rh-positive or Rh-negative blood. If they have Rh-negative blood, their blood is checked for Rh antibodies and the father's blood type is determined. If he has Rh-positive blood, Rh sensitization is a risk. In such cases, the blood of pregnant women is checked for Rh antibodies periodically during the pregnancy. The pregnancy can proceed as usual as long as no antibodies are detected.

If antibodies are detected, steps may be taken to protect the fetus, depending on how high the antibody level is. If the level becomes too high, amniocentesis may be performed. In this procedure, a needle is inserted through the skin to withdraw fluid from the amniotic sac. The level of bilirubin (a yellow pigment resulting from the normal breakdown of red blood cells) is measured in the fluid sample. If this level is too high, the fetus is given a blood transfusion. Usually, additional transfusions are given until the fetus is mature enough to be safely delivered. Then labor is induced. The baby may need additional transfusions after birth. Sometimes no transfusions are needed until after birth.

As a precaution, women who have Rh-negative blood are given an injection of Rh antibodies at 28 weeks of pregnancy and within 72 hours after delivery of a baby who has Rh-positive blood, even after a miscarriage or an abortion. The antibodies given are called Rh_0(D) immune globulin. This treatment destroys any red blood cells from the baby that may have entered the bloodstream of the women. Thus, there are no red blood cells from the baby to trigger the production of antibodies by these women, and subsequent pregnancies are usually not endangered.

Fatty Liver of Pregnancy: This rare disorder occurs toward the end of pregnancy. The cause is unknown. Symptoms include nausea, vomiting, abdominal discomfort, and jaundice. The disorder may rapidly worsen, and liver failure may develop. Diagnosis is based on results of liver function tests and may be confirmed by a liver biopsy. The doctor may advise immediate termination of the pregnancy. The risk of death for pregnant women and the fetus is high, but those who survive recover completely. Usually, the disorder does not recur in subsequent pregnancies.

Peripartum Cardiomyopathy: The heart's walls may be damaged late in pregnancy or after delivery, causing peripartum cardiomyopathy. The cause is unknown. Peripartum cardiomyopathy tends to occur in women who have had several pregnancies, who are older, who are carrying twins, or who have preeclampsia. In some women, heart function does not return to normal after pregnancy. They may develop peripartum cardiomyopathy in subsequent pregnancies. These women should not become pregnant again. Peripartum cardiomyopathy can result in heart failure which is treated.

Problems with Amniotic Fluid: Too much amniotic fluid (polyhydramnios) in the membranes containing the fetus (amniotic sac) stretches the uterus and puts pressure on the diaphragm of pregnant women. This complication can lead to severe breathing problems for the women or to preterm labor.

Too much fluid tends to accumulate when pregnant women have diabetes, are carrying more than one fetus (multiple pregnancy), or produce Rh antibodies to the fetus's blood. Another cause is birth defects in the fetus, especially a blocked esophagus or defects of the brain and spinal cord (such as spina bifida). About half the time, the cause is unknown.

Too little amniotic fluid (oligohydramnios) can also cause problems. If the amount of fluid is greatly reduced, the fetus's lungs may be immature and the fetus may be compressed, resulting in deformities; this combination of conditions is called Potter's syndrome.

Too little amniotic fluid tends to develop when the fetus has birth defects in the urinary tract, has not grown as much as expected, or dies. Other causes include the use of angiotensin-converting enzyme (ACE) inhibitors, such as enalapril or captopril, in the 2nd and 3rd trimesters. These drugs are given during pregnancy only when they must be used to treat severe heart failure or high blood pressure. Taking non-steroidal anti-inflammatory drugs (NSAIDs) late in pregnancy can also reduce the amount of amniotic fluid.

Placenta Previa: Placenta previa is implantation of the placenta over or near the cervix, in the lower rather than the upper part of the uterus. The placenta may completely or partially cover the opening of the cervix. Placenta previa occurs in 1 of 200 deliveries, usually in women who have had more than one pregnancy or who have structural abnormalities of the uterus, such as fibroids.

Placenta previa can cause painless bleeding from the vagina that suddenly begins late in pregnancy. The blood may be bright red. Bleeding may become profuse, endangering the life of the woman and the fetus.

Ultrasonography helps doctors identify placenta previa and distinguish it from a placenta that has detached prematurely (placental abruption).

When bleeding is profuse, women may be hospitalized until delivery, especially if the placenta is located over the cervix. Women who bleed profusely may need repeated blood transfusions. When bleeding is slight and delivery is not imminent, doctors typically advise bed rest in the hospital. If the bleeding stops, women are usually encouraged to walk. If bleeding does not recur, they are usually sent home, provided that they can return to the hospital easily. A cesarean section is almost always performed before labor begins. If women with placenta previa go into labor, the placenta tends to become detached very early, depriving the baby of its oxygen supply. The lack of oxygen may result in brain damage or other problems in the baby.

Placental Abruption (Abruptio Placentae): Placental abruption is the premature detachment of a normally positioned placenta from the wall of the uterus. The placenta may detach incompletely (sometimes just 10 to 20%) or completely. The cause is unknown. Detachment of the placenta occurs in 0.4 to 3.5 per cent of all deliveries. This complication is more common among women who have high blood pressure (including preeclampsia) and among women who use cocaine.

The uterus bleeds from the site where the placenta was attached. The blood may pass through the cervix and out the vagina as an external hemorrhage, or it may be trapped behind the placenta as a concealed hemorrhage. Symptoms depend on the degree of detachment and the amount of blood lost (which may be massive). Symptoms may include sudden continuous or crampy abdominal pain, tenderness when the abdomen is pressed, and shock. Premature detachment of the placenta can lead to widespread clotting inside the blood vessels (disseminated intravascular coagulation), kidney failure, and bleeding into the walls of the uterus, especially in pregnant women who also have preeclampsia. When the placenta detaches, the supply of oxygen and nutrients to the fetus may be reduced.

Doctors suspect premature detachment of the placenta on the basis of symptoms. Ultrasonography can confirm the diagnosis.

Problems with the Placenta

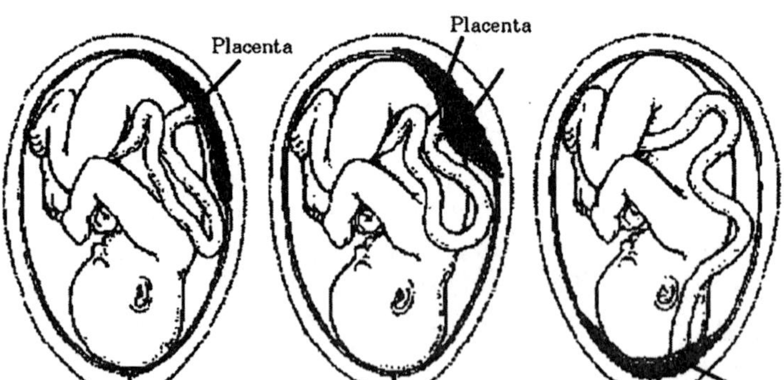

Normally, the placenta is located in the upper part of the uterus, firmly attached to the uterine wall until after delivery of the baby. In placental abruption (abruptio placentae), the placenta detaches from the uterine wall prematurely, causing the uterus to bleed and reducing the fetus's supply of oxygen and nutrients. Women who have this complication are hospitalized, and the baby may be delivered early. In placenta previa, the placenta is located over or near the cervix, in the lower part of the uterus. It may cause painless bleeding that suddenly begins late in pregnancy. The bleeding may become profuse. The baby is usually delivered by cesarean section.

Women with premature detachment of the placenta are hospitalized. The usual treatment is bed rest. If symptoms lessen, women are encouraged to walk and may be discharged from the hospital. If bleeding continues or worsens (suggesting that the fetus is not getting enough oxygen) or if the pregnancy is near term, an early delivery is often best for the woman and the baby. If vaginal delivery is not possible, a cesarean section is performed.

Prenatal Development: The Miracle of Life

Unfortunately, the process of conception does not always work smoothly. For some couples infertility is a major concern.

This provides information about what happens after the two sex cells unite to create a person. It describes some of the many factors and concerns associated with pregnancy, *prenatal development*, and the neonate. We hope the information will help you gain some knowledge of the most precious thing any of us can be a part of: the miracle of life.

Physical Development Highlights

- By the 25th day of development the heart begins to beat and the embryo is one-hundredth of an inch in length
- At four weeks of age the embryo has limb buds that will become the arms and legs
- Ten weeks after conception the embryo is now termed a fetus

- The ability of the fetus to kick, swallow, and sleep is present at sixteen weeks

- A 24 week old fetus can respond to sound

- At the 28th week of development the fetus has lungs that can breathe air, and its eyes are open

- After 38 weeks the "baby" is full term and ready to be born

Growth Trends

- Cephalocaudal-growth from the head to the feet (which is why a baby's head is disproportionate to his/her body)

- Proximodistal-growth from the center to the limbs

The physical development of the human fetus is a complex and fascinating process. Learn more! Check out these related sites.

Various Aspects of Fetal Development

During prenatal development, the fetus also develops cognitively. There is new evidence that suggests one's intellectual abilities can be positively influenced during the fetal and infant life stages.

Hazards to Prenatal Development

The fetus is not immuned from the outside world. In fact, some things can be damaging to the unborn child. These are called teratogens, and often result in birth defects. They include such things as maternal disease, poor nutrition, stress, pollutants, and cigarette smoking. Some of the most troubling teratogens are *alcohol* and *drugs*.

It is critical to the development of the fetus that expectant mothers avoid teratogens, and receive good prenatal care. Other prenatal hazards involve genetic birth defects.

Prenatal Diagnosis

Types of Tests Used...

Ultrasound (Sonography)

- Ultrasound uses high frequency sound waves directed into the abdomen. The echo from the sound is produced into pictures on a monitor
- This type of testing can be used to find fetal weight, length, position, number of fetuses, and various physical features or abnormalities

Amniocentesis

- This is a medical procedure in which a sample of the amniotic fluid is withdrawn with a syringe
- The fluid is tested for chromosomal abnormalities, as well as metabolic disorders.
- It is done between the 12th and 16th week of pregnancy
- Learn more about *amniocentesis*

Chorionic Villus Sampling (CVS)

- In this procedure a sample of the placenta is taken between the 8th and 11th week.
- The results usually take about 10 days, and can show chromosomal abnormalities.

Maternal Blood Test

- This also can be referred to as alpha-fetoprotein
- The blood test can be done in the 14th to 20th week
- Neural tube defects can be detected with this type of testing

Types of Abnormalities during Pregnancy

Down Syndrome: This is a situation where there are three of the 21st chromosomes, rather than the normal pair. Downs includes mental retardation and physical deformities to varying degrees. Some of the physical differences are a round face, protruding tongue, short limbs, and motor deficiency. Many people with Down Syndrome can live fairly normal and active lives. Maternal blood tests, CVS, and amniocentesis can be used to detect Downs.

Sickle Cell Disease and Anemia: This is when a person's red blood cells (RBC) are crescent shaped (instead of disk-shaped). An abnormal RBCs cause problems with that person's ability to use oxygen, and therefore can be a very deadly disease. Sickle Cell is mainly found in African Americans. Testing for Sickle Cell includes amniocentesis and CVS.

Anecephaly: Anecephaly is a very devastating neural tube disorder, which causes brain and skull malformation. Most children die at birth. Ultrasound and amniocentesis are used in diagnosis.

This was only meant to give the reader a very brief description and introduction to the vast world of prenatal diagnosis. Others abnormalities include Cystic Fibrosis, Tay-Sachs disease, spinabifida, Turner's syndrome, and PKU. These are only a few of the many abnormalities that are detected every day by prenatal diagnosis.

Taking Care of Yourself

A major part in a baby's development is directly linked to the mother. To ensure that the baby stays healthy and continues normal development, you may have to make some changes. Pregnant women are encouraged not to use drugs, alcohol, or nicotine as this can seriously affect the baby's development. As a mother you should avoid drinking caffeinated beverages such as coffee and soda while increasing water consumption. Though this all may seem difficult, you are taking an active part in keeping your baby healthy.

Exercising is also very important when pregnant. Although, while exercising, there are many warnings you must heed to prevent any injury to either you or your child.

Some tips on what you should avoid in exercising while pregnant:

- Don't begin a workout without a warm up
- Don't exercise flat on your back, it can decrease the blood flow to your uterus
- Don't get dehydrated or overheated
- Don't get too fatigued

Some Safe Sports to Pursue During Pregnancy

- Walking a 12-15 minute mile
- Swimming, because you are using your arms and legs, but the water is supporting your weight is a great exercise to do while pregnant
- Tennis is acceptable, but balance may be a problem
- Golf and bowling are also good recreational exercises, but they do nothing to condition the heart. In these, as in tennis, you may find you have some difficulty in keeping your balance

As a mother-to-be, it is important to learn more about keeping you and your baby healthy.

Definitions of Heredity

The handing down of certain traits from parents to their offspring. The process of heredity occurs through the genes.

- The transmission of characters from parent to offspring by information encoded in the parental germ cells. Genealogy, the transmission of characteristics from one generation to the next
- The sum of the qualities and potentialities genetically derived from one's ancestors; the relation between successive generations, by which characteristics persist
- The genetic transmission of characteristics from parent to offspring
- Resemblance among individuals related by descent; transmission of traits from parents to offspring. The transmission of physical and emotional traits and characteristics from parents to offspring. The passing of traits from parents to offspring
- Genetically transmitted or transmittable from parent to offspring; relating to inheritance or heredity
- The tendency to develop depression may be inherited; there is evidence it runs in families
- The theosophical philosophy explains heredity as being the attraction of reimbodying monads to the respective families with which they have affinities of various kinds; and thus it is the reimbodying egos carrying such individual characteristics or attributes which perpetuate them in the family life-stream. It is the sutratman (life thread) which runs through successive generations
- Science of passing traits from parents to young
- Passed on through family lines. Refers to conditions that are passed on from generation to generation

- The transmission of a trait, such as blue eyes, from parents to offspring
- The process of transmitting biological traits from parent to offspring through genes, the basic units of heredity. Heredity also refers to the inherited characteristics of an individual, including traits such as height, eye colour, and blood type
- The transmission of qualities from parent to offspring through the genes. Also see inherit. The process that brings about similarities for parent and offspring, and for several offspring of the same parent
- The biological process whereby genetic factors are transmitted from one generation to the next
- The total of inherited attributes
- Heredity is a 1985 album by Rational Youth, now down to singer Tracy Howe with numerous studio musicians. In retrospect, Howe was less than happy with the album, especially with the fact that it looked like he was using the Rational Youth name as a flag of convenience for a solo album. To date, the album has never seen a CD release
- Heredity is a scientific journal concerned with heredity in a biological sense, i.e. genetics
- Heredity (the adjective is hereditary) is the transfer of characters from parent to offspring, either through their genes or through the social institution called inheritance (for example, a title of nobility is passed from individual to individual according to relevant customs and/or laws).

Mendel's Law of Heridity

Gregor Mendel was born July 22, 1882 in Heizendorf Austria. He was an Austrian monk who found actual proof of the existence of genes, and is considered to be the father of genetics. His work was relatively unappreciated until the early 1900ís.

Mendel changed his name when he entered into the Augustinian Monastery in Brno, Austria. There he became an ordained priest in 1847, and in 1851 he entered into the University of Vienna to train to be a teacher of mathematics and Biology. Gregor failed the elementary teacher exam and returned to Brno in 1845. After failing.

The teacher exam, he became a teacher at technical high school, where he thought mathematics, natural science, and science. During the end of Mendelís life in 1868, Mendel was promoted in the monastery to abbot. He died on January 6, 1884.

During the middle of Mendelís life, Mendel did groundbreaking work into the theories of *heredity*. Using simple pea pod plant, Mendel studied seven basic characteristics of the pea pod plants. By tracing these characteristics, *Mendel discovered three basic laws,* which governed the passage of a trait from one member of a species to another member of the same species.

The first law states that the sex cells of a plant may contain two different traits, but not both of those traits.

The second law stated that characteristics are inherited independently from another (the basis for recessive and dominant gene composition).

The third law states that each inherited characteristic is determined by two hereditary factors (known more recently as genes), one for each parent, which decided weather a gene is dominant or recessive. In other words, if a gene is recessive, it will not show up within the plant, however the dominant trail will). Mendelís work and theories, later became the basis for the study of modern genetics, and are still recognized and used today.

Another scientist who also used to work with genes was McClintock, he proposed that gene can move between chromosome site. He was born in 1886 and died in 1937. He also used to be An American Geneticist Barbara.

Gregor Mendel is accorded a special place in history of genetics. His experiments beautifully designed, were the first to focus on the numerical relationships among traits appearing in the children or offspring hybrid and his interpretation, clear and concise, was based on material hereditary elements that undergo segregation and independent assortment. Poignantly overshadowing the creative brilliance of mendels work is the fact that it was virtually ignored 34 years. Only after the dramatic rediscovered in 1900s, 16 years after Mendelís death was rightfully recognized as the founder of genetics. Mendel discovered the heredity traits are determined by cellular elements.

If we think Mendel today, without him no one would be discovered the scientific laws of plants and animal heredity. This law described how traits such as eye colour in human beings and tallness in plants are passed on from generation to generation.

According to mendels records, he saw clearly that there was a prediction pattern by which plant traits were passed from generation to generation. This pattern had never been reported before. He explained his patterns in principles, or rules, that we know as the *Mendelian law of heredity*.

Mendelís experiments and conclusion may be briefly sketched, and he obtained pairs of different varieties of pure breeding yellow peas, each pair differing in one easily diagnosed trait.

Mendel based his rules on an important idea. This idea was that the hereditary traits depend on a single factor. Each factor behaved independently, and it controlled a single trait. Each factor also remained "pure" or unchanged, from generation to generation. Even when the trait was not visible, the factor for that trait was unchanged and the trait could reappear in a later generation.

Definition-laws of Heredity Formulated by Mendel: The laws of heredity formulated by Mendel to explain the transmission of characteristics from one generation to the next. There are two laws, the **Law of Segregation** and the **Law of Independent** Assortment.

Gregor Mendel approached problem-solving in new and different ways.

1. He worked with pure strains of garden peas. The flowers have both male (stamen-anther and filaments) and female (pistil-stigma, style and ovary) reproductive parts. He removed (emasculated) the male part (anthers and filaments that produce the male sex cells) so he could control the way each plant was fertilized. This was done artificially by mechanically transferring the male sex cells from the desired plant to the stamen of the emasculated plant. The offspring using this procedure are referred to as "crosses".

2. He only worked with traits of the peas that could easily be seen. He experimented using only one trait at a time. Traits included, (a) stem length, (b) flower colour or (c) seed shape.

3. Mendel kept detailed records of his "crosses". He counted the pea offspring and calculated, *using* mathematics, how often the trait occurred in the offspring.

Unit Factors (Genes)

- Mendel believed that traits were determined by individual units called factors

- He believed that each offspring received a factor from each parent

- Today these factors are called genes

- He guessed that each trait, such as flower colour, would be determined by a pair of genes

- He speculated that offspring plants who receive the trait (gene) from each parent of red flower colour will be a pure strain (purebred) of red colour flowers

Mendel's Law of Dominance

- Even though each of the F1 Generation plants received a gene for red colour from one parent and a gene for white colour from the other parent (i.e., hybrid plants), the white colour did not express itself

- Mendel concluded that the gene for red colour is dominant over the gene for white colour because all the flowers of the F1 Generation were red

- He also concluded that the gene for white colour was recessive (white colour could not be expressed) because white flowers DID NOT appear in the F1 Generation. To be expressed, a recessive gene would have to pair with another recessive gene

- In genetics today the composition of the genes of a plant or mammal (red/red; white/white; and red/ white) is called the genotype (the type of genes). The expression of genes to what we see (red coloured flowers; white coloured flowers; and red-coloured flowers) is called the phenotype (the type of physical expression-literal meaning "the form that is shown") [Review the biochemistry of phenotypic expression- see below # 4]

- Letters are used to describe a gene. The DOMINANT red-coloured flower gene = R (upper case letter); The RECESSIVE white-coloured flower gene = r (lower case letter). Therefore a white-colored purebred flower would have the genotype, rr. The red-coloured purebred flower would have the genotype RR. The genotypes RR and RR are said to be homozygous (two of the same kinds of genes). The RR genotype is homozygous dominant. The RR genotype is homozygous recessive. Another popular name for a gene is allele. An allele in this example is R or r. When talking about the gene pair RR or RR, one can use the words allelic pair

- The Punnet square of the cross of the white-coloured flower purebred plants with the red-coloured flower purebred plants is described in the animation below. The red, RR genotype parent (red-colored flower) is crossed with the RR genotype (white-coloured flower) parent

By convention the dominant genes are written first (RR) except when visualizing the genotypes after the female and male sex cells unite. Having two or more different genes in the genotype of the F1 generation creates a heterozygous genotype (at least one dominant and one recessive).

Since R is dominant, Mendel hypothesized, the phenotype (physical expression of the genotype) is red-coloured flowers.

Mendel went the next step. Based on what he knew, he hypothesized that crossing two plants of the F1 generation would result in an F2 generation containing (in every 4 plants) approximately one homozygous dominant red-coloured flower plant, one homozygous recessive white-coloured flower plant and two heterozygous red-coloured flower plants. Or in other words 3 red-coloured flower plants to 1 white-colored flower plant. This he confirmed with mathematical data of thousands of offspring. With his data he arrived at his First Law.

Mendel's Law of Segregation

- Mendel guessed that the TWO genes for flower color separate or segregate, when the sex cells form during meiosis.

- In the case of the hybrid pea flowers (RR), each plant would have one gene (allele) for red colour (R) and one gene (allele) for white colour (r).

- These two genes would separate or segregate from each other during the formation of the sex cells. About half of the sex cells would receive the gene for red colour and the other half the gene for white colour.

Mendel's Law of Segregation States : The two genes that determine a particular trait will separate when sex cells form. Half of the cells will receive one gene (allele) and half of the cells will receive the other gene (allele) of the allelic pair. *During meiosis, the parental genotypes are segregated to the sex cells (parental gametes).*

Co dominance, not only for flower colour in snapdragons but also for many human proteins. The proteins produced by BOTH alleles are expressed.

For example, alpha1-antitrypsin is a protein present in the fluids and blood serum of the body. It's purpose is to prohibit the destruction of proteins by other enzyme—"eating" proteins. Each human has two alleles or genes for each trait.

Homozygous normal is MM. In this situation the person has large quantities of this protease inhibitor (alpha1-antitrypsin). Protease is the general name for a protein-degrading protein. Human alpha1-antitrypsin moves through a gel across an electric current at a medium speed. Homozygous abnormal is ZZ. This person has extremely low levels of alpha1-antitrypsin. This person has hardly any protease inhibitor and is at risk of getting emphysema. The protein in this person moves VERY slowly in the same electric field, more slowly than any other genetic form of the inhibitor (thus the use of the last letter of the alphabet).

If an MM male and a ZZ female get married, all their children will have an MZ genotype. Both proteins (intermediate and slow migrating) will be seen... they both are expressed. In other words, they are both dominant.

A dominant gene or allele is found in each generation, however, a recessive gene or allele skips one generation. Think of the pea flower examples: RR × RR = RR × (the original parents were white and red. In the F1 generation, there were no white).

F1 cross: RR x RR = RR, RR, RR, RR (F1 parents were only red and white showed up again in the F2 generation

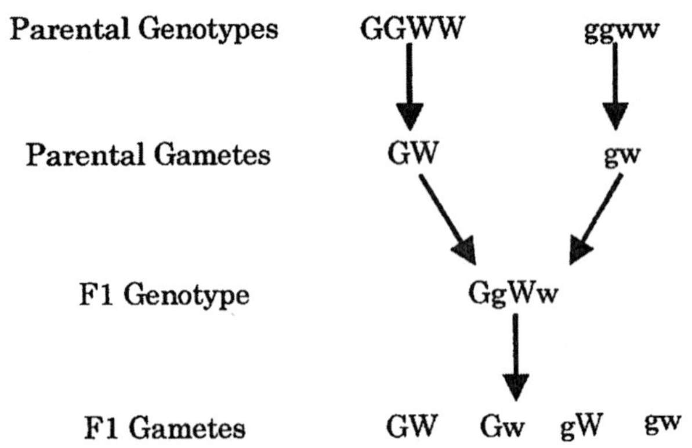

Mendel's Law of Independent Assortment: The inheritance of genes (alleles) that control one trait is NOT affected by the inheritance of the genes that control a different

trait. Allelic (gene) pairs that control different traits separate independently of one another.

Chromosome Theory of Heredity	*Mendelian Theory of Heredity*
1. Chromosomes occur in pairs.	1. Mendelian factors occur in pairs
2. Paired chromosomes separate during meiosis. Each sex cell (gamete) receives only one chromosome of the pair.	2. Mendel's paired factors separate during meiosis. Each sex cell (gamete) receives only 1 factor of the pair.
3. Chromosome pairs separate independently of other chromosome pairs during meiosis.	3. Mendel's factor pairs separate independently of other factor pairs.
4. Individual chromosomes return to their original paired numbers in the fertilized egg.	4. Mendel's individual factors become paired factors in the offspring.

Sex Determination

The inheritance of abnormal genes found on the 22 pairs of human chromosomes (autosomes) obey the principles of Mendelian genetics. The inheritance of abnormal genes on the X-chromosomes also are based on Mendel's principles.

Gender issues complicate this process only in regard to the Y chromosome. Males have only one X-chromosome whereas females have a pair of X-chromosomes. The expression of genetic abnormalities in the offspring of affected people takes on a new dimension when the Y-chromosome is included in the "equation".

XY = male; XX = Female;

Female X-chromosome represents an abnormal gene on that particular chromosome. The lower case "a" means it is a recessive gene (allele).

FROM THE DATA

There is a 50 per cent chance that the couple will have a girl or a boy.

There is a 50 per cent chance that a daughter will be born who is a carrier for the trait (does not have the effects of the genetic abnormality...just carries the abnormal gene). (Remember: The female has two X-chromosomes. The other chromosome has a normal gene-dominant. In a heterozygous situation, the recessive gene is suppressed and the person is normal but is a carrier).

There is 50 per cent chance the couple will give birth to a boy with the genetic abnormality (*Note*: A recessive trait is expressed only in males in sex-linked inheritance because of the absence of a dominant gene. The gene for this trait is not present on the Y-chromosome. As a result, it acts as if it were a homozygous recessive with the male expressing the genetic abnormality). In the female, the extra X-chromosome produces the normal product and compensates for the chromosome with the abnormal gene.

What would happen if the abnormal recessive gene were on the X-chromosome of the male (meaning the father has the genetic abnormality), instead of on one of the female X-chromosomes.

Answer: Sons will not possess the abnormal trait, so they will be normal but all daughters born to the couple will be CARRIERS.

XY = male; XX = Female; the red superscript "a" on the female and male X-chromosomes represent an abnormal gene on those particular chromosomes.

This represents the cross between a sister who is a carrier and brother who expresses the genetic abnormality (consanguineous marriage can also be cousins) and illustrates why this kind of marriage is not permitted by law.

There is a 50 per cent possibility of having a boy with the genetic abnormality. This person would be like a homozygous recessive.

There is a 50% chance of the daughters to be born with the genetic abnormality and an equal chance for the daughter to be a CARRIER.

A consanguineous marriages increase the incidence of genetic abnormalities.

XY = male; XX = Female

The female X-chromosome represent an abnormal gene on those particular chromosomes. The normal gene of the allelic pair is on the other X-chromosome. Since the defect is expressed by a dominant gene, the mother would have the genetic abnormality. Like the Mendelian example, the mother would have a heterozygous dominant genotype (Aa).

Dominant genes are expressed in this genotype and thus the mother has the genetic abnormality.

Daughters have a 50 per cent chance (1 in 2) of receiving the dominant allele and expressing the genetic abnormality.

Likewise, sons have the same risk as the daughters. The affected son would have the genetic abnormality.

What would happen if the "a" gene would be on the X-chromosome of the father rather than on one of the X-chromosomes of the mother? Try it using a punnet square before you look at the answer.

Answer: 100 per cent of the daughters would receive the dominant allele and have the genetic abnormality. None of the sons would receive the gene. They would be normal.

3

Neonate Development

Definitions of Neonate

The word infant derives from the Latin in-fans, meaning unable to speak. It is commonly used as a slightly more formal word for baby (the youngest category of child). A newborn infant is known as a neonate (neonatal) after the final stage of gestation.

- A newborn infant, animal or baby, typically up to four weeks of age, or a newly born or hatched individual.
- Term used to refer to newborn metatherians. A term used to describe a newborn infant from birth to 1 month of age kitten between zero and two weeks old.
- An infant from birth to 4 weeks (28 days) of age.

The Neonate

In nature, the mother's Colostrum and milk is the only external source of everything required by the neonate, except for air it breaths. The neonate is constantly and rapidly changing, both structurally and physiologically. In the uterus, the fetus is living in a warm, moist, protected environment, and receiving all its needs from the mother. Major metabolic and physiological changes occur in the transition from a fetus to the newborn.

Physiological Changes in Neonate

At birth, most neonates—

- Have limited fat stores
- The fat stores which are present are not readily available for metabolism
- Use up their limited glycogen stores rapidly after birth
- Have poor gluconeogenic capacity (synthesis of glucose by the liver)
- Are agammaglobulinemic (they have very low concentrations of immunoglobulin in their blood)
- Neonate have low iron stores
- Have structurally immature intestines
- Have immature digestive capabilities,
- Low activities of all pancreatic enzymes
- Low activities of stomach pepsin
- Low activities of many intestinal enzymes
- Immature stomach acid generating mechanism
- High rennin activity—for precipitation of casein, curd formation in the stomach
- Increasing lactase activity—for breakdown of lactose in the intestine
- High salivary lipase activity—for breakdown of milk triglycerides

In addition, the composition of mammary gland secretions is constantly changing, particularly over the initial 3 to 5 days postpartum. There is considerable inter- and intra-species variation in how the Colostrum changes during the initial days after parturition.

So, there is an effect of mammary function on neonate survival and vitality, and an effect of the neonate on mammary function.

Intestinal Absorption of Immunoglobulin

Normally we think of ingested food as being degraded in the digestive tract and digestion products being absorbed into the animal. For example, proteins would be degraded to amino acids or small peptides and those are absorbed. However, for a short time after birth most mammals will absorb macromolecules intact. This is particularly important for absorption of colostral immunoglobulins which would be rendered inactive if digested. In most species this absorption occurs by a non-specific pathway (not receptor mediated) where macromolecules are taken into the intestinal absorptive cells (enterocytes) by formation of tubules at the base of the apical microvilli. These tubules pinch off in the cell to form small vesicles that can transport the contents to the basolateral membrane and release their contents into the extra cellular space. From there the macromolecules can be absorbed into the blood. This process of macromolecule absorption only occurs in the jejunum, not in the ileum. Macromolecules are taken up into ileal enterocytes, but are degraded in lysosomes within the cell. In those cases where intestinal absorption is not selective, most anything will be absorbed including carbon aggregates and plastic. Therefore, there is little discrimination in absorption of the different immunoglobulin.

Intestinal transport of macromolecules is extensive but not selective in some species (such as the bovine, porcine and canine neonate), while in others (human infants, pigs, rabbits) there is little intestinal absorption of macromolecules at all. In the latter cases, maternal immunoglobulins are transported to the fetus before birth and the neonate is born with high concentrations of immunoglobulin in the blood.

The process of macromolecular absorption is initially high at the first suckling, then declines gradually. Intestinal closure to uptake of macromolecules has occurred when no more intact macromolecules can be absorbed. Intestinal closure is a continual, gradual process that starts immediately after birth and proceeds until there is no longer transport of macromolecules. Time of closure is the time after birth when macromolecules (including immunoglobulins) can no longer pass from the intestinal lumen, through the intestinal cell and into the neonate's vascular system. Closure is complete in the calf by about 24 hr after birth, in the piglet at about 36 to 48 hr, in the foal at about 24 to 48 hr, in cats and dogs at about 24 to 48 hr.

Relationship between closure, IgG absorption, colostral IgG, and calf serum IgG.

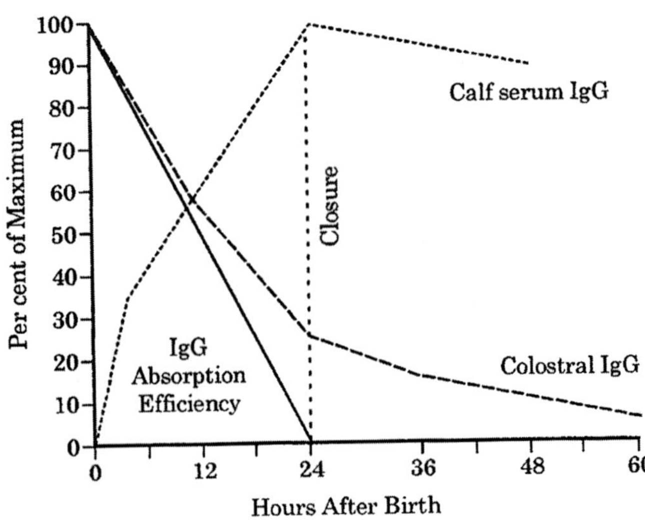

Colostrum Formation

Composition of the mammary secretion at the first milking or the first suckling reflects the functional changes that have occurred in the gland up to that time. These functional changes include the secretions resulting from the two stages of lacto genesis, as well as other functional changes in the epithelial cells occurring in concert with lacto genesis, such as selective transport of immunoglobulin. After repeated milk removal, the composition of the mammary secretions changes rapidly over the initial 2 to 3 days after parturition, so that there is a continuous transition of composition from Colostrum to mature milk. All components of the mammary secretion are changing during this transition period.

Study of the hormonal control of mammary differentiation around the time of parturition mostly has focused on lacto genesis, and specifically on the synthesis of lactose and/or the expression of casein and lactalbumin genes and secretion of those proteins. However, a great deal is occurring in the mammary gland that ultimately results in the formation of Colostrum.

Intestinal Protective Factors in Colostrum and Milk

Several factors found in milk may function in the neonate's digestive tract to minimize the potential for enteric disease. These include:

Immunoglobulin: Even after closure the immunoglobulin in milk may protect the intestinal lumen. Immunoglobulins are relatively resistant to digestion. IgA is of particular interest in the human infant because it is the major immunoglobulin in human milk.

Lactoferrin: The iron-binding capacity of lactoferrin gives it bacteriostatic and bactericidal properties. Lactoferrin is high in human milk, low in cow milk.

Lysozyme: May degrade the cell wall of some bacteria and allow them to be lysed. Lysozyme is high in human milk, but there is essentially none in cow milk. Lysozyme can act in concert with IgA, lactoperoxidase and ascorbate to lyse bacteria.

Lactoperoxidase: Uses hydrogen peroxide and halogens (I, Cl) to halogenate proteins and make them inactive. Also causes per oxidation of substances. The lactoperoxidase system also includes an interaction of the enzyme with thiocyanate. Lactoperoxidase activity is ~20 fold lower in human milk than cow milk, but the human infant also secretes considerable lactoperoxidase in the saliva.

Milk Cells: Generally the leukocytes in normal milk (in the absence of mastitis) are macrophages. These cells probably retain some of their phagocytic abilities when ingested into the neonate. However, a role for these cells in the neonate has not been completely described.

Gut Flora: One of the best mechanisms for protecting against digestive tract infections is the establishment of the proper intestinal flora. In human milk there is a carbohydrate growth factor which stimulates the growth of Lactobacillus bifidus. The high lactose concentration, low protein content, low bulk and low buffering capacity of human milk also encourages L. bifidus growth. The high lactose content means that lactose is still available for bacterial fermentation in the intestine, resulting in an acidic environment which reduces viability of many potentially pathogenic bacteria. Although similar factors to the Bifidus factor have not been identified in milk of other species, there may be other milk factors that contribute specifically to the establishment of the optimal microbial flora in the digestive tract.

Bioactive Factors in Colostrum and Milk

Nutrient Sources

Milk Fat Globule

- Fat Soluble Vitamins

- Steroid Hormones
- Progesterone less than 1 to more than 30 mg/ml whole milk
- Estrogens Estradiol-17ß-peaks in Colostrum is ~.6 mg/ml, then declines
- Estrone-peaks in colostrum is 2 mg/ml, then declines
- Corticosteroids ~3 mg/ml at parturition,.2-.5 mg/ml in milk
- Androgen Low concentrations

Casein: Provides a balanced source of amino acids.

- In addition to a nutritional source of amino acids, partial digestion of ß-casein; yields **casomorphins**-Tyr-Pro-Phe-Pro-Gly-Pro-Ile
- These pepides have opioid activity in several assays
- Generally are protease resistant
- Have been identified in calf blood after milk ingestion
- May regulate development of the intestinal mucosal immune system in the neonate

Other immunomodulatory activities have been identified in peptides generated by proteolytic hydrolysis of ß-lactoglobulin and □-lactalbumin.

Enzymes

Milk and colostrum contain many enzymes. There is considerable species variation. Some have fairly high activities in some species.

High in cow milk, low in human milk:

Lactoperoxidase

Xanthine oxidase

Ribonuclease

Alkaline Phosphatase

High in human milk, low in cow milk:

Lipase activity (bile salt activated)

Lysozyme

Protease activity

Milk and colostrum also contain plasmin and plasminogen, and plasminogen activator activity, as well as trypsin inhibitor activity.

Carrier Proteins in Colostrum and Milk

- Vitamin-binding proteins
- Mineral-binding proteins
- Lipid-binding proteins
- ß-lactoglobulin; binds fatty acids, retinol (?) serum albumin binds fatty acids
- Hormone-binding proteins
- Corticosteroid-binding globulin

Hormones in Milk

A wide range of hormones have been identified in milk, including:

- Prolactin is in cow milk
- Growth hormone is in milk

- GHRH is in human milk
- Somatostatin is in milk
- Thyroid hormones
- Insulin is in milk
- Melatonin
- Relaxin

Conclusion

In addition to supplying nutrients and factors directly involved in protection against pathogens, colostrum and milk contain a many components that may affect the growth and development of the neonate. These include:

Enzymes growth factors

Carrier proteins

Immunoglobulins

Hormones

Immunomodulators

Steroid

Leukocytes

Protein

Intestinal protective factors

Peptide

Psychological Impacts

In medical circles, neonatal circumcision was long assumed to be psychologically begin. It was believed that newborn infants had "poorly developed" neurologic systems; that newborns could not feel pain; or, if they did feel the pain, they would not remember it. According to that orthodoxy, the experience of neonatal circumcision could never have any lasting effect on a child and could not traumatize a child.

- The belief that infants cannot feel pain is now outmoded and discredited.

It was also a common belief that the foreskin had no particular structure and no useful function; and that the patient would never later regret its loss.

- The idea that the foreskin is a "useless flap of skin" is contradicted by a modern understanding of anatomy.
- The assumption that no patient would ever regret being circumcised was not justified.

Enough evidence now exists to say with confidence that male circumcision causes psychological changes. The trauma of the experience is injurious. It can have long-term deleterious effects later in life. However, the specific psychological and behavioural changes resulting from early genital trauma have never been properly investigated. Much more study is needed to further elaborate these changes. The study of the psychology of circumcision can be divided into several interrelated areas:

- The effects of pain and prenatal trauma on the child
- Grieving the loss of a body part
- Effects of early trauma and loss in the adult
- The effects on the parent (parental-infant bonding)
- The effects on society

- Factors influencing parents and doctors to request or perform circumcisions

Types of Birth

1. Home Birth
2. Hospital Birth
3. Water Birth
4. Caesarean Section
5. Instrumental Deliveries
6. Induced/Accelerated Labour
7. Twins and Multiple Births

Home Birth

Your midwife will stay with you throughout your labor if you give birth at home, whereas in hospital, she is likely to be caring for several women in labor at the same time, and so cannot give you her undivided attention. Other reasons why people choose home birth are:

- Because you feel more relaxed in your own home
- You can eat and drink as you please
- You can move around as you please
- And make as much noise as you please!
- You can learn to breastfeed in private
- No queues for the bath or toilet!
- Less noise at night
- No visiting times unless you set them!

You can also have whoever you like with you—partner, mum, sister, children—and your baby will be born into a warm and welcoming environment rather than the impersonal atmosphere of a hospital.

You might also choose a home birth because you don't want to have any medical interventions in your labor or pain-relieving drugs.

When women labor at home, they don't need nearly so much pain relief. The pain is more manageable at home.

The Facts on Home Birth and How They Affect You

At the start of the 20th century, 99% of British babies were born at home. By the 1980s, the rate had dropped to less than 1%. Nowadays, the percentage is a little higher-2.2% at the end of the 1990s. However, women's access to a home-birth service varies greatly between areas and is restricted by the attitudes of health care providers.

The Safety of Home Birth

For normal, low-risk women, research shows that home birth is as safe as hospital birth and results in less intervention, and less morbidity (illness) for mothers and babies.

In the past, evidence on the safety of planned home birth has been obscured because outcomes for all out-of-hospital births were amalgamated. Many of these are unplanned home births—premature babies born suddenly, or concealed pregnancies born after no antenatal care, often with no midwife present. Outcomes from such births are often poor and have little in common with a planned home birth, with facilities for transfer to hospital if necessary. A summary of the issues surrounding place of birth published by the UK's National Prenatal Epidemiology Unit found that: "There is no evidence to support the claim that the safest policy is for all women to give birth within hospital. For some women it is possible, but not proven, that the iatrogenic risks associated with institutional delivery may be greater than any benefit conferred."

The evidence-based maternity care bible, A Guide to Effective Care in Pregnancy and Childbirth, says: "Several methodologically sound observational studies have compared the outcomes of planned home births (irrespective of the eventual place of birth) with planned hospital births for women with similar characteristics. A meta-analysis of these studies showed no maternal mortality and no statistically significant differences in prenatal mortality between the groups. The number of births included in the studies was sufficiently large to rule out any major difference in prenatal mortality risk in either direction."

The British Medical Journal published several large studies on home birth safety in one single issue in 1996. Its editorial concluded that home birth was "safe for normal, low-risk women, with adequate infrastructure and support". Planned home birth is associated with better outcomes for both mothers and babies. The National Birthday Trust Fund's study of home birth in the UK covered nearly 6,000 planned home births in 1994/95. Each woman was matched for risk level and obstetric history with another who planned a hospital birth. The study found that:

- The home birth group had roughly half the risk of ending up with a Caesarean section, compared with the hospital group
- The home birth group had roughly half the risk of ending up with a ventouse or forceps delivery
- Mothers who planned home births were less likely to suffer a post-partum hemorrhage
- Babies in the planned home birth group were significantly less likely to be in poor condition at birth

- Babies in the planned home birth group were less likely to suffer birth injuries

How Many Women Really Want Home Births? Who are They?

However, interest is likely to be higher in areas where home birth is seen as a realistic option and where women know others who have given birth at home. One midwifery group working on an under-privileged estate in South London has a 43% home birth rate. A local midwife commented that "the biggest element of 'persuasion' comes, not from the midwives, but from other women".

The home birth rate varies greatly between trusts—from over 20% of births in some areas, to less than 1% in others. Although differences in local demand will account for some of the discrepancy, it is likely that attitudes of health care providers have more influence. Some simply fail to present home birth as a real option, while others actively discourage it.

Women choose home births for reasons varying from a desire to avoid interventions in childbirth, to avoiding separation from older children. Some have had bad experiences in hospital, while others had uneventful hospital births and simply do not see the need to have subsequent children there. In areas where home birth is well supported, it is certainly not restricted to the well-off, as the South-East London Midwifery Group has shown.

When the time comes to have your baby, you have a number of choices: You might choose home to give birth at home if:

- You think you will feel more at ease there

- You do not want an epidural

- You want to be certain of having a midwife with you through your labor
- You don't want to leave other children
- You want to give yourself the best chance of a vaginal delivery.

You might choose a birth centre or midwifery unit if:

- You prefer not to see doctors
- You want a homely atmosphere
- You would like to be with other women.

You might choose hospital if:

- You or your baby have medical problems
- You want an epidural
- You feel comforted by technology
- You would like some time away from the family in order to focus on your baby

Pain in Labour

There are a range of options:

- Self-help methods that enable you to manage the pain and reduce your perception of it. These include positions, breathing, massage, reflexology, aromatherapy, warm water and TENS
- Drug-based methods that relax you—and so reduce your perception of pain. These include Entonox, pethidine and diamorphine
- Methods that block the pain messages from reaching your brain, e.g. epidural anaesthetics

You can give birth

- Standing
- Squatting
- On all-fours (good for a breech birth)
- Lying on your side
- Half-sitting
- In the water
- On the floor
- On a bed.

You can let your labor start on its own or (if you are going overdue) use natural induction methods, such as sex (see induced/Accelerated Labour). You might leave your waters to break on their own or your midwife might break them for you.

You may want to pick your baby up yourself after birth or you might prefer the midwife to wrap your baby up and give her to you

You will need interventions if you have certain medical conditions such as pre-eclampsia or placenta pelvic.

Hospital Birth

So useful questions to ask are:

- Can I move around during labor, or do I have to stay on the bed?
- Do you monitor the baby's heartbeat continuously, or intermittently during labor? Do you use fetal scalp electrodes regularly? (the kind of monitor that clips onto your baby's head).

- Will you break my waters at a certain stage in labor?
- Is it all right for me to eat and drink as I please during labor, or will I be allowed only water?
- Can I wear my own clothes for labor?
- How many people can I bring with me to support me during labor?
- Have you got a birthing pool and midwives experienced at water birth?
- Do you have a 24-hour epidural service, or are epidurals only available in office hours?
- Can I give birth in any position I choose?
- Will there be student doctors or midwives present at my birth?
- What is your induction/caesarean section/forceps/ ventouse rate? How does this compare with other local hospitals?
- How long will I stay in hospital after the birth?
- What are visiting hours? Can my partner visit me outside these hours?
- How many women are breastfeeding when they leave the hospital?

Make an appointment to visit the Delivery Suite and see the rooms there. Ask yourself whether this is the place you would like your baby to be born? See if there is a bean bag and birthing ball in each room, and whether there are comfy chairs. Decide whether the rooms are designed for the benefit of midwives, or for laboring women. The answer to these and the questions outlined above will give you a good idea of how woman-centred the hospital is.

Water Birth

Research shows that women who labor in water often have shorter labors. Many women find that the water itself is enough to help them through contractions and they don't need other forms of pain relief. You're less likely to need a forceps or ventouse delivery if you spend some of your labor in water and some studies show you're less likely to tear.

Benefits

- The warm water helps you relax
- And makes you buoyant so that you can easily change position
- And gives a sense of privacy and control

Remember that you don't have to give birth in the pool. You can use it just for the first part of labor, and then get out when you want to push. Most midwives prefer you to deliver the placenta 'on dry land'.

Safety

You might worry that your baby will breathe in water if she is born in the pool. Most authorities agree that the baby will not start to breathe until she comes into contact with air. It's important to bring the baby to the surface of the water as soon as she is born.

Some time ago, there were fears about the temperature of the water in the pool affecting babies adversely. However, there's no sound evidence that this has ever been a problem. The best advice is to keep the water between 35°C and 37°C.

If you are planning to use a birthing pool in hospital:

- Find out how likely it is that the pool will be available when you want it (and a midwife experienced in delivering babies this way)
- Check out hospital policies on pool-use

If you are hiring a pool for use at home:

- Take advice from your midwife or a member of the local NCT or the Active Birth Centre on who to hire from
- Practice putting the pool together, filling it and using it BEFORE you go into labor!

Caesarean Section

Why might you need a caesarean?

It might be because:

- Your baby's exit is blocked by the placenta (placenta praevia)
- Your baby is large in relation to your pelvis
- Or isn't growing properly
- Or you have a serious medical condition

You don't always have to give birth by caesarean if you fall into one of these categories, but your consultant might well suggest an ELECTIVE CAESAREAN which means that a date is fixed for your operation before you go into labor.

You might need an EMERGENCY CAESAREAN if monitoring before or during labor shows your baby is in distress.

What happens when you have a caesarean?

Before the operation, you will have to:

- Sign a consent form
- Remove your jewellery
- Take out your contact lenses

Drink some medicine to neutralize the acid in your stomach

You will have a couple of centimeters of pubic hair shaved off, a drip put into your arm, a catheter into your bladder and heart monitors fixed to your chest.

Your anesthetic will either be a local (spinal or epidural) which means that you'll be awake for the operation, or a general. General anesthetics aren't very common nowadays.

There will be around eight doctors, midwives and other staff assisting at your caesarean. You won't be able to see anything because there will be a screen across your chest. The surgeon makes the cut on the 'bikini line' (the scar won't show when your pubic hair grows back). It takes about ten minutes for your baby to be delivered and during this time you will hear the clinking sound of surgical instruments and lots of sucking noises as the amniotic fluid is suctioned out. You'll feel strange (not painful) sensations—as if someone is rummaging around inside you! After your baby is born, the pediatrician will check him over and then he will be given to you to cuddle while your operation is completed which takes about 40 minutes.

After Your Caesarean

After you have had a caesarean it is important not to compare recovery with friends who have had vaginal births. Remember that you have had major abdominal surgery and think of getting better in terms of weeks rather than days.

Pain

During the operation you may have been given strong morphine-like painkillers but you will need more pain relief after the surgery.

You may be offered pain-killing injections (morphine-like drugs that will make you feel dopey)

- A small pump containing strong pain-relieving drugs you can operate yourself
- Suppositories
- Tablets
- A TENS machine.

If you are in pain, ask for help and more, or different, painkillers.

Other Treatment

You will have a drip in during surgery which will usually be left in for some time afterwards and you will be monitored carefully over the next day or two.

You will have had a catheter inserted to keep the bladder emptied, which may be left in place for 24 hours after the operation.

You may need iron tablets.

You may have a lot of trapped wind and this can be uncomfortable. Because of the surgery, it will be difficult to stand upright at first. Try standing bent over at first, and gradually get more upright day by day. It can get very ache and you will feel tired for some time. However, you will be encouraged to get up and move around to improve circulation and recovery. (Ask for help if needed)

You shouldn't lift anything heavier than your baby for about six weeks and you won't be able to drive either for about six weeks, depending on your insurance

Making Yourself Comfortable

- To get out of bed-wriggle to the edge of the bed and draw your knees up to your chest. Using your hands, push yourself into a sitting position. When you are sitting on the side of the bed with your legs touching the floor, and feel steady, stand up

- Whether sitting or lying, experiment with pillows to support you and your baby so that you're both comfortable
- Keep the pressure off your scar with high-waist knickers
- Some people find peppermint tea (or ginger) helps release trapped wind
- Ring your bell and ask for help if you are in pain and when you need to reach or hold your baby

Your Feelings

It may help for you to understand why you had a caesarean. In most cases, it will have been due to a specific problem which will not affect future births. It may help to ask you midwife to go through your notes with you so you know exactly what happened. You can ask for a copy of your notes to take home.

Instrumental Deliveries

Instrumental deliveries are carried out using forceps or ventouse. You might need some help to give birth if:

- You have been pushing for a long time
- You are exhausted
- Your baby's heartbeat shows signs of distress

Forceps

Forceps look like stainless steel salad servers and the curved ends, which cradle your baby's head, are called 'blades'. If you do not already have an epidural in place, you will be given a local anaesthetic to make sure that you feel nothing. Your midwife will help you put your legs up in stirrups and the doctor will make a cut (episiotomy) through the back of your vagina to enlarge the opening. He then places the forceps gently round your baby's head. When you have your next contraction, you push and the doctor pulls to bring your baby into the world.

Most doctors are experienced with forceps, but a forceps delivery may still bruise your baby's head, damage your bladder, and mean that having sex is uncomfortable for some time after the birth. So you might choose the ventouse instead

Ventouse

The ventouse is a small silicone plastic cup attached to a vacuum device. Suction is gradually applied to remove the air from the cup and make it adhere to your baby's head. You will probably not need an episiotomy for a ventouse delivery so you will find it less traumatic than forceps. However, it can take 7-10 minutes to apply the suction and sometimes the cap slips off the baby's head and has to be reapplied. The top of your baby's head will be swollen for a few days after her birth. Not all doctors are experienced with ventouse

Induced/Accelerated Labour

Why an induction?

Your labor might need to be started if:

- You are 10 days or more past your due date and the placenta is failing
- You have pre-eclampsia (raised blood pressure and protein in your urine)
- Your baby is not growing well
- Your waters break, but after 24 hours, you're still not having contractions
- You have diabetes

Methods of Starting Labor

Natural methods (at home) include curry, a long walk and sex! Artificial methods (in hospital) include:

- Prostaglandin pessaries or gel, placed in the vagina to soften the cervix and make it ready for labor
- Breaking the waters round the baby, using an instrument like a long crotchet hook
- A syntocinon (artificial oxytocin) drip

The method chosen depends on the state of your cervix and your consultant obstetrician's preference.

While there may be very good reasons for inducing your labor artificially, there are some risks to be aware of. Induction might: make your labor very long or very quick and sudden contractions may be difficult to cope with.

Induction might also stress your baby and is more likely to lead to a forceps or ventouse delivery than a non-induced labor.

Monitoring

Your midwife will need to monitor your baby's heart constantly if you have a syntocinon drip, but intermittent monitoring should be fine if you have had pessaries or your waters broken.

Remember you don't always have to be lying down to be monitored. Ask to be monitored while you are sitting in a chair, or even kneeling on the floor.

Accelerating Labor

If your labor is very slow, you might be asked whether you would like to have your waters broken, or even a syntocinon drip, to speed it up. If you're happy to continue as you are, and your baby is fine, tell your midwife that you want to leave things alone.

Twins and Multiple Births

Having twins is unusual, but if you are healthy and your pregnancy is normal, you can expect to give birth vaginally without medical intervention, if you wish.

Your hospital may have policies on the delivery of twins—for example, on monitoring or inducing labor. Expecting twins does make medical problems such as high blood pressure more likely and twins often arrive before their due date.

However, there is no evidence that inducing your labor is helpful. Monitoring two babies' hearts using a hand held sonic aid it just as appropriate as electronic monitoring for twins, if things are progressing smoothly.

Moving around, standing up and feeling able to follow your body's instincts is as important if you are having twins as it is in a singleton birth.

Students and other medical staff may want to be present at the birth. However, three midwives (one for you and one for each baby) are all you need. If the babies are being born earlier than 38 weeks or are expected to arrive in poor condition, you may need a paediatrician for each baby and if medical complications arise during labor, you may need an obstetrician.

With twins, the first stage of labor follows the same pattern as for a single baby, but may go more slowly. You can choose all the pain relief options available (see Pain Relief).

The babies will be born one at a time. After you have given birth to your first baby, the midwife will check the position of the second baby. If he is head-down you will be able to go on to give birth again. If the second baby is in the breech position, you may be offered a forceps delivery to help this baby out quickly.

Rarely, the second baby is lying awkwardly and if it is not possible to manipulate him or her into a better position, a caesarean is your only option.

The third stage of labor proceeds in the same way as with a singleton pregnancy. If the twins are identical, there will be one placenta, but if they are non-identical, two placentas will be expelled after both births.

The Neonate or the New Born

The birth of a child is a momentous and life altering event. It certainly changes the family dynamics.

Normal Newborn Weights and Measurements

- Weight: 7-8 lbs
- Length: 19-21 inches
- Vision: 20/40-vision is clear at a 12 inch distance

Neonatal Testing

The Apgar Scale: Within the first five minutes after birth the infant is assessed for his or her general health.

Evaluations

- Heart rate
- Respiratory effort
- Muscle tone
- Body color
- Reflex irritability

Scoring

- The infant receives a score of 0, 1, or 2 for each of the above-mentioned health signs. This is performed by a obstetrician or nurse.
- Results
  - 7-10 = normal or good condition
  - 5 = may have developmental difficulties
  - 3 or below = doubtful survival

The Brazelton Scale: The newborn is assessed hours after birth.

Evaluations

- Neurological development
- Various reflexes
- Reactions to people in different circumstances

Scoring

27 tests are broken down into four categories:

- Physiological
- Motoric
- State
- Interaction

Results of the test are shown by terms such as: "worrisome", "normal", or "superior".

Developmental Changes in Both Mother and Child

Introduction

Whatever the reason, the birth of a child is a major event. It changes a lot in the family dynamics. The whole family system that you are accustomed to is about to change to make room for one more! After you have found that special someone and made a commitment to one another, the next step might be to create a family. This step not only affects the new baby, but the mother, father and the grandparents. In having a child, your family circle has added a few more chapters to its book. This page will help you better understand some of the changes that can occur when you decide to add on to your family. It will help you recognize some common concerns of parents and grandparents, and will help both mothers and fathers recognize what they might be feeling.

Changes in the Mother

What does a mother expect to happen to her emotions once the baby comes?

Having a baby is an exciting time for a mother-to-be, but the body goes through a lot of hormonal, mental and physical changes. If one is not prepared for what will happen to their bodies and state of mind, the joyous moment of having a baby could easily turn into a stressful event.

Hormones

There are certain hormones that have great effect on a mom-to-be. Estrogen and progesterone, the female sex hormones, rise to a higher level during pregnancy. This is a normal event in the woman's body. Once the baby is born they then plummet. This sudden change is normal, but so are some of the emotional effect it has on some women. One important thing to understand when going through this change is that you are not the only one this happens to. Hormonal changes is just one of the many things occurring in a mother-to-be's body. There are ways to treat some unwanted feelings that can be triggered by these changes. Check with your doctor.

Physical Effects

With all of the hormonal changes, there are also some physical changes that occur during and after pregnancy.

During pregnancy body changes include weight gain as well as beginning to lactate, or produce milk. Gaining weight is a normal process in pregnancy and the average weight gain is 25 to 30 pounds. The female body also starts to lactate in order to provide nutrition for her new baby.

The female body also has many other physical changes that can occur here are just a few that are common:

- Constipation
- Hemorrhoids
- Vaginal Discharge
- Low Backache
- Varicose Veins
- Fatigue
- Dizziness
- Cramps
- Indigestion
- Nausea
- Some Swelling

This might seem over whelming, but there are available treatments to help reduce these occurrences, and in time most of them will disappear.

Emotional Effects

"Baby Blues" and Depression

"The baby blues is a relatively mild form of sadness and anxiety that begins soon after the childbirth and may last for several weeks." Approximately 50 to 75 per cent of women experience this. This emotional occurrence is nothing to worry about and will soon disappear.

Postpartum depression is a disorder that is fairly common. Most mothers don't understand the disorder and often it goes undiagnosed. It is important for women to express any feelings that are bothersome. Let your family know exactly how you feel. An estimated 10 to 20 per cent of women experience some form of depression after giving birth. In order to be a little bit more prepared how to pick out some warning signals here are a few signs:

- Nervousness and anxiety
- Sluggishness, exhaustion
- Sadness, hopelessness
- Poor concentration, memory loss, confusion
- Over-concern for baby
- Uncontrollable crying
- Feeling of guilt or inadequacy
- Fear of harming self or baby (Feelings After Birth)

Most of these emotions will go away on their own, but in some cases medical intervention should be considered.

Providing Developmental Care

Remarkable medical advances in the NICU have resulted in the survival of extremely fragile infants who are vulnerable to a variety of adverse, brain-based outcomes. This is due in large part to the experiential effects of life in the NICU during a highly sensitive period of brain development. Research has shown that individualized, developmentally supportive care can significantly improve both short and long term outcomes for prematurely born infants. This session will provide an overview of the principles and practice of developmentally supportive care. A focus on intervention will highlight the implementation of individualized, behaviourally guided practice. An understanding of relationships as the organizing focus of all early development will be empha Infants in a Neonatal ICU experience the most rapid brain development that they will have at any time in their lives. Development occurs along a continuum, with the usual course being interrupted by the birth of a preterm newborn. When an infant is born prematurely, the sequencing of neonatal sensory development is influenced by the NICU experience. Stimuli, as well as the neonate's early use of disordered systems, become factors that may lead to developmental problems. This pre-conference will explore the development of neonatal sensory systems and its affect on our practice as caregivers in the NICU. Explore the multidisciplinary continuum of care from delivery to discharge, and beyond "What is your role?" Don't miss this opportunity to further your NICU's commitment to providing developmentally supportive care sized.

The largest and most important neurodevelopment in the early stages of the life of the fetus include the basic structure of the brain, the development of the nerve tracks, the development of the sensory organs, and the basic connections and pathways. These all occur purely by the genetic encoding of the cells in the central nervous system and the genetically driven biochemical processes that guide it.

In the second stage of development, the basic structure of the eyes and ears with their pathways into central nuclei and then to the cortex is genetically-driven. The visual and auditory cortex areas will develop in anticipation of need and without stimulation. However, how they develop and what they are capable of responding to in later life is influenced by the stimuli that they receive during certain periods of their development. These sensory organs are genetically developed but environmentally modified. In the third stage of development, the processes are almost entirely driven by responses to stimulation or use of the environment of the architectural setting, even though the process was originally structured by genetics. New pathways, memory circuits, and the whole range of new connections for the neurons in the cortex of the brain are made in response to stimuli.

The Sequence of Sensory Development

The sensory systems of the human fetus develop in sequence. Four of them (called the somatesthetic modalities) including touch, pain, position, and temperature sensitivity are the first to appear in the fetal life. These are followed very shortly be "vestibular modalities" ... the sensory systems of the middle ear that detect motion. The third systems to develop and begin to function are the chemosensory systems of smell and taste. These are all well established with connections to the midbrain and basal ganglion in the second trimester of fetal life. The sensory auditory modalities, which include responses to sound and vibration, appear early in the third trimester, followed by visual development. It is interesting to observe that at this point in development the human fetus has no need for light or visual stimuli to have perfectly normal visual development. When an infant is born prematurely (prior to term), the sequencing of sensory development becomes an issue since stimuli and use of systems that are out of sequence can create developmental problems, i.e. visual development can begin before the auditory modalities are in place.

The concept of a "critical period" is based on a biological fact that there is a period of time when external stimulation results in changes in the location and relationship of neurons in the cortex. There is clearly a critical period in visual development, as well as auditory development, for humans. The critical period in visual development is initiated with the first visual exposure after birth. Combinations of light and images initiate a biochemical process which stimulates the neurons of the optic cortex to move into 'column' relationships based on the visual image. This critical period in visual development occurs primarily during the first five or six months after birth. During this time, the infant develops the neuron relationships that allow it to perceive lines and shapes in subsequent life. It is called a critical period because the movement of the neurons cannot occur after this critical period is passed. The critical period can be delayed by being reared in a dark environment. The exact time of the onset of the critical period in premature (or preterm) infants in not known.

The auditory critical period begins at or around 32 weeks gestations (about eight weeks before birth). It continues in the first and probably into the second year of life. The most important periods are the earlier months when the auditory stimuli result in changes in the auditory nucleus. The critical period is essential for the development of frequency discrimination, and pattern recognition. These are established early in the infant's life. Interference with hearing systems during this critical period can result in changes in the auditory function. The children are not deaf, they just have decreased ability to discriminate frequencies and to recognize patterns (in sounds).

One type of sensory interference occurs when stimuli are out of sequence or when their intensity is inappropriate for the stage of development. Either circumstance will produce interference in the normal sensory development process. The most common examples of sensory interference are the early introduction of visual stimuli before auditory patterns are learned and in place. Examples in animals have shown that the introduction of visual stimuli before auditory patterns are in place will interfere with both the frequency discrimination and pattern recognition. Early introduction of visual stimuli to newborn puppies will interfere with both auditory discrimination and with chemosensory discrimination, particularly smell.

This raises serious concerns for chemosensory, auditory and visual development in premature infant settings in the NICU because many of the stimuli are either at inappropriate levels or out of sequence for the normal development processes. There is no evidence that premature birth accelerates or alters the sequence of development for the fetus. There continues to be a sequence in the sensory developmental processes with smell and taste preceding auditory development, which in turn precedes visual development. Certain markers of neurological functions occur at precisely the same time outside the uterus as inside. However, the infant's neuroprocesses are either at or slightly delayed from those that a fetus would have had in utero. The differences are small, and are primarily related to sensory discrimination and pattern recognition in either hearing or vision.

Once the visual processes have been initiated, the infant needs to have a clear image and varying levels of light, otherwise there is an increased rate of growth of the eye and the development of myopia. Therefore, the environment of the infant is going to need faces and/or objects within a distance which produces a sharp image, and the correct amount of light for seeing the image.

Light is a source of energy and capable of producing injury under a variety of circumstances. The risk of damage from light is related to the wavelength, the intensity, the duration, characteristics of the eye, the maturation of the eye and the eyelids, etc. Clearly the eye is designed to receive light and can for brief periods tolerate fairly intense light. But, the eye also needs periods of very reduced light for retinal regeneration. This means that lighting cycles in a nursery must be controlled to provide periods for the infant's retinal regeneration.

Most NICU units have large banks of overhead lights that produce high levels of illumination and are difficult to control. It is clear that what is called for is individually controlled lighting for all infants. Through the use of focused lighting and dimmer controls, it must be possible to individualize the light levels for each infant according to their stage of development.

Outside daylight is another concern. When the outside window exposure is such that direct sunlight can hit the infant, then they are at risk for high levels of light intensity far above those normally experienced in a nursery. Infants must be protected from such exposure.

Many NICU units are very noisy places. The general level of equipment noise, air-handling units, monitoring equipment, communications systems, all contribute to the ambient noise level. As the noise level rises, the staff noises and voice levels will also rise.

Infants exposed to constant high levels of background noise have been shown to have two major long-term negative effects. The first is interference with development of frequency discrimination. The bandwidth for the reception of sound in the ear actually increases or widens (in a noisy environment) so that the infant, as a child and as an adult, will be less able to discriminate between frequencies. For example, perfect pitch (which can be important to a musician) would be impossible.

The addition of sound absorbing surfaces and removal of sound reflecting surfaces does assist in noise control, but it is not effective without active reduction in sound production. Incorporating silent alarms (such as blinking lights), paging systems with vibrators rather than beeping sounds, and a variety of other substitutions can eliminate a lot of current noise generators.

There are a wide range of benefits from lack of intrusive activities during sleep periods, which suggests providing a way to segregate infants so they are not disturbed by events in neighbouring cribs or general events within the NICU.

Motor and Sensory Development

Images of the fetus 'walking' and 'thumb-sucking' have come as a surprise to the public, but such movements have, for several years, been well described in the literature. For those working in obstetrics and ultrasonography, these pictures are therefore remarkable only in their definition and real-time technology. There is no doubt that the fetus has complex movements, but what does it all actually mean?

Images showing the fetus taking steps are not surprising to paediatricians. Newborn infants can be shown to 'walk' when held upright on a flat surface. Even preterm infants can do so a short time after birth. Many of the behaviours demonstrated by the newborn in the early postnatal period, are a function of primitive reflex activity, dependent on the development of spinal reflex arcs which are not under control of the brain and are complete in the fetus as early as eight weeks' gestation. Reflexes are very different from purposeful voluntary movements which develop during the first year of life. Such movements are dependent on the maturation of the central nervous system, and in particular on myelination, which starts from around 18 weeks' gestation. In fact, all primitive reflexes have to be lost before voluntary movement can be mastered. Reflex activity usually disappears in normal babies by about eight months of age but may persist in those with neurological damage.

Most of what is known about fetal behaviour has been learned since the introduction of ultrasonography in the 1950s. The fetus exhibits a wide range of behaviours starting with slow flexion and extension of the spine and limbs at around 7.5 weeks' gestation. The variety of movements increases rapidly over the next 3-4 weeks and many different movement patterns have been described including breathing, truncal rotation, limb flexion/extension, sucking and yawning. As the fetus progresses towards term the movements become more regular and coordinated as a result of increased maturation of the nervous system.

Fetal thumb-sucking can be demonstrated as early as 12-14 weeks' gestation. Preference for sucking a particular thumb *in utero* has been shown to predict head position preference in the newborn and subsequent right or left-handedness. Handedness was thought to be dependent on cerebral lateralisation. However, fetuses prefer one thumb to another from as early as 12 weeks' gestation, well before the brain has any control over movement. This early sucking behaviour is likely to be under reflex control. Stimulation of the brain is known to influence brain organisation and it is argued that this reflex activity may eventually stimulate the brain to develop 'handedness' and subsequent lateralisation of function.

Sensory development in the fetus has been studied mostly in response to sound, and hearing can be shown as early as 23 weeks' gestation. Fetuses respond with a slowing of the heart rate during maternal speech. There is evidence to suggest that fetuses can differentiate between different speech sounds and show preference for the maternal native language. It may be that experience of speech prenatally begins the process of acquiring language postnatally.

Fetal Learning and Memory

Fetal learning can be observed in studies of 'habituation'. Habituation is the decrement in a particular behavioural response that occurs when a new stimulus is presented repeatedly. In an environment of constant sensory stimulation, the ability to ignore meaningless stimuli is essential for the efficient functioning and survival of the fetus. Although very simple, it is one of the most widespread methods of learning and there is good evidence that habituation reflects a healthy nervous system. Habituation of the human fetus has been studied mainly in response to sound and has been shown as early as 23 weeks' gestation. Stimulation using other sensory modalities such as taste and smell, which are functional at earlier ages, may reveal habituation occurring even earlier in pregnancy. Studies have shown fetal habituation to be predictive of cognitive function in early childhood.

Other aspects of fetal memory have been investigated. Babies whose mothers consistently rested in front of a popular television programme during pregnancy became alert, stopped moving and showed slowing of their heart rate a few days after birth when the theme tune of the programme was played. This behaviour was not shown by babies whose mothers had not watched this programme during pregnancy. This indicates that the fetus is able to learn and remember familiar auditory stimuli, and retain this information over the birth period.

Clinical Implications

The behaviour of the fetus can be argued to represent the functioning and integrity of its nervous system. By building up a picture of 'normal behaviour' of the fetus it is possible to determine the well-being of the fetus. Different fetal behaviour has been observed in pregnancies complicated by maternal smoking or recreational drug abuse, fetal abnormality and in pregnancies which later spontaneously aborted.

Interest in the causes of cerebral palsy has led many researchers to conclude that most brain damage happens before labour. A recent study from Edinburgh showed that most infants who had neurological symptoms and who died in the newborn period had evidence of brain damage occurring during pregnancy. No obvious cause could be found when the pregnancy was reviewed. Routine ultrasound imaging in pregnancy now occurs throughout the developed world. The development of 4-dimensional ultrasound may eventually provide detailed information about the normality of fetal behaviour. Measurements of the quantity and quality of fetal movement may allow us to determine the severity and extent of any neurological damage if present. The more severely injured the nervous system, the greater the differences in behaviour from a fetus with an intact nervous system. The identification of fetuses exhibiting such behavioural patterns may offer insight into the pathoaetiology of intrauterine brain injury and allow optimal management of these pregnancies.

Birth Injury

What is a Birth Injury?

Occasionally during the birth process, the baby may suffer a physical injury that is simply the result of being born. This is sometimes called birth trauma or birth injury.

What Causes Birth Injury?

A difficult birth or injury to the baby can occur because of the baby's size or the position of the baby during labor and delivery. Conditions that may be associated with a difficult birth include, but are not limited to, the following:

- Large babies–birth weight over about 4,000 grams (8 pounds, 13 ounces)
- Pre-maturity-babies born before 37 weeks (premature babies have more fragile bodies and may be more easily injured)
- Cephalopelvic disproportion—the size and shape of the mother's pelvis is not adequate for the baby to be born vaginally
- Dystocia—difficult labor or childbirth

- Prolonged labor
- Abnormal birthing presentation—such as breech (buttocks first) delivery

What are some of the more common birth injuries?

The following are common birth injuries:

Caput Succedaneum

Caput is a severe swelling of the soft tissues of the baby's scalp that develops as the baby travels through the birth canal. Some babies have some bruising of the area. The swelling usually disappears in a few days without problems. Babies delivered by vacuum extraction are more likely to have this condition.

Cephalohematoma

Cephalohematoma is an area of bleeding underneath one of the cranial bones. It often appears several hours after birth as a raised lump on the baby's head. The body resorbs the blood. Depending on the size, most cephalohematomas take two weeks to three months to disappear completely. If the area ofbleeding is large, some babies may develop jaundice as the red blood cells breakdown.

Bruising/Forceps Marks

Some babies may show signs of bruising on the face or head simply as a result of the trauma of passing though the birth canal and contact with the mother's pelvic bones and tissues. Forceps used with delivery can leave temporary marks or bruises on the baby's face and head. Babies delivered by vacuum extraction may have some scalp bruising or a scalp laceration (cut).

Subconjunctival Hemorrhage

Sub-conjunctival hemorrhage is the breakage of small blood vessels in the eyes of a baby. One or both of the eyes may have a bright red band around the iris. This is very common and does not cause damage to the eyes. The redness is usually absorbed in a week to ten days.

Facial Paralysis

During labor or birth, pressure on a baby's face may cause the facial nerve to be injured. This may also occur with the use of forceps for delivery. The injury is often seen when the baby cries. There is no movement on the side of the face with the injury and the eye cannot be closed. If the nerve was only bruised, the paralysis usually improves in a few weeks. If the nerve was torn, surgery may be needed.

Brachial Palsy

Brachial palsy occurs when the brachial plexus (the group of nerves that supplies the arms and hands) is injured. It is most common when there is difficulty delivering the baby's shoulder, called shoulder dystocia. The baby loses the ability to flex and rotate the arm. If the injury caused bruising and swelling around the nerves, movement should return within a few months. Tearing of the nerve may result in permanent nerve damage. Brachial palsy is treated with immobilization of the arm with a brace or splint. Special exercises are also used to help maintain the range of motion of the arm.

Fractures

Fracture of the clavicle or collarbone is the most common fracture during labor and delivery. The clavicle may break when there is difficulty delivering the baby's shoulder or during a breech delivery. The baby with a fractured clavicle rarely moves the arm on the side of the break. There may be bruising over the broken bone. Simply immobilizing the arm and shoulder is the recommended treatment and healing begins quickly.

Prematurity

Prematurity is the condition of being born before a full gestation. The duration of an average human gestation (length of pregnancy) is 40 weeks from conception to "term." Term etymologically means "end" but in this context has become synonymous with parturition or delivery. A premature birth is often referred to as preterm. A premature infant is sometimes informally called a premie.

- Premature infants are at a higher risk for plagiocephaly since the cranial bones become stronger and harder in the last 10 weeks of pregnancy. Also, since many premature infants spend extended periods of time in the neonatal intensive care (NICU) unit on a respirator, their heads are maintained in a fixed position, increasing the risk for this condition. Birth before 37 weeks' gestation

- The condition of a fetus weighing between 1,000 and 2,499 grams

- Underdevelopment; the condition of an infant born too soon. Refers to infants delivered before 37 weeks from the first day of the last menstrual period

Once a baby is born, he or she needs to breathe continuously to get oxygen. In a premature baby, the part of the central nervous system (brain and spinal cord) that controls breathing is not yet mature enough to allow non-stop breathing. This causes large bursts of breath followed by periods of shallow breathing or stopped breathing. The medical term for this condition is apnea of pre maturity.

Apnea of pre maturity is fairly common in preemies. Doctors usually diagnose the condition before the mother and baby are discharged from the hospital, and the apnea usually goes away on its own as the infant matures. Once apnea of pre-maturity goes away, it does not come back. But there's no doubt about it—it's frightening while it's happening.

What is Apnea of Prematurity?

Apnea is a medical term that means a baby has stopped breathing. Most experts define apnea of prematurity as a condition in which premature infants stop breathing for 15 to 20 seconds during sleep.

Generally, babies who are born at less than 35 weeks' gestation have periods when they stop breathing or their heart rates drop (The medical name for a slowed heart rate is bradycardia). These breathing abnormalities may begin after 2 days of life and last for up to 2 to 3 months after these premature infants are born. The lower the infant's weight and level of prematurity at birth, the more likely it is that the infant will have AOP spells.

Although it's normal for all infants to have pauses in breathing and heart rates, those with AOP have drops in heart rate below 80 beats per minute, which causes them to become pale or bluish. They may also appear limp, and their breathing may be noisy. They then either start breathing again by themselves or require help to resume breathing.

AOP may happen once a day or many times a day. Doctors will closely evaluate your infant to make sure the apnea isn't due to another condition, such as infection or internal bleeding.

Apnea of prematurity should not be confused with periodic breathing, which is also common in premature newborns. Periodic breathing is marked by a pause in breathing that lasts just a few seconds and is followed by several rapid and shallow breaths. Periodic breathing is not accompanied by a change in facial color (such as blueness around the mouth) or a drop in heart rate. A baby who has periodic breathing resumes regular breathing on his or her own.

Although it can be frightening, periodic breathing typically causes no other problems in newborns.

How is Apnea of Prematurity Treated?

Most of the time, premature infants (especially those less than 34 weeks' gestation at birth) will receive medical care for apnea of prematurity in the hospital's Neonatal Intensive Care Unit (NICU). When they are first born, many of these premature infants must get help breathing from a ventilator because their lungs are too immature to allow them to breathe on their own.

During mechanical ventilation, a tube is placed into the baby's trachea (windpipe) and breaths of air are blown through the tube into the baby's lungs. These breaths are given at a set pressure. The ventilator is also programmed to give a certain number of breaths per minute, and the baby's breathing, heart rate, and oxygen levels are continuously monitored.

Sometimes babies with apnea of prematurity are given medications to help mature their lungs and allow the preemies to come off mechanical ventilation within a few weeks and breathe on their own.

When infants are disconnected from a mechanical ventilator, often they require a form of assisted breathing called nasal Continuous Positive Airway Pressure (CPAP). A nasal CPAP device consists of a large tube with tiny prongs that fit into the baby's nose, which is hooked to a machine that provides oxygenated air into the baby's air passages and lungs. The pressure from the CPAP machine helps keep a preemie's lungs open so he or she can breathe. However, the machine does not provide breaths for the baby, so the baby breathes on his or her own.

Once preemies are off a mechanical ventilator and breathing on their own—with or without nasal CPAP—they are monitored continuously for any evidence of apnea. The cardiorespiratory monitor (also known as an *apnea* and *bradycardia*, or A/B, monitor) also tracks the infant's heart rate. An alarm on the monitor sounds if there's no breath for a set number of seconds. When the monitor sounds, a nurse immediately checks the baby for signs of distress. False alarms are not uncommon.

If a baby doesn't begin to breathe again within 15 seconds, a nurse will rub the baby's back, arms, or legs to stimulate the breathing. Most of the time, babies with apnea of prematurity spells will begin breathing again on their own with this kind of stimulation.

However, if the nurse handles the baby, and the baby still hasn't begun breathing on his or her own and the baby becomes pale or bluish in colour, oxygen may be administered with a handheld bag and mask. The nurse or doctor will place the mask over the infant's face and use the bag to slowly pump a few breaths into the baby's lungs. Usually only a few breaths are needed before the baby begins to breathe again on his or her own.

If a baby begins to have many such apnea spells, medication is sometimes given intravenously or by mouth to stimulate the part of the brain that controls breathing. This often reduces the apnea spells.

Caring for Your Child

Apnea of prematurity usually resolves on its own with time. For most preemies, this means AOP stops around 44 weeks of post-conceptional age. Post-conceptional age is defined as the gestational age (how many weeks of pregnancy at the time of birth) plus the postnatal age (weeks of age since birth). In rare cases, AOP continues for a few weeks longer.

Healthy infants who have had AOP usually do not go on to have more health or developmental problems than other babies. The apnea of prematurity does not cause brain damage. If a healthy baby is apnea free for a week, he or she will probably never have apnea again.

Although sudden infant death syndrome (SIDS) does occur more often in premature infants, no relationship between AOP and SIDS has ever been proven.

Aside from AOP, there may be other complications with your premature baby that may limit the time and interaction that you can have with your child. Nevertheless, you can bond with your baby in the NICU. It's a good idea to talk to the NICU staff about what type of interaction would be best for your baby, whether it's holding, feeding, caressing, or just speaking softly. The NICU staff is not only trained to care for premature babies, but also to reassure and support the parents of preemies.

4

Methods of Child Development

So many methods are involved in child development for understanding, recording and interpreting behaviour of children. These methods are well designed, subjective and objective procedures. Many methods are developed in child development to observe child behaviour and collect information, describe, measure and make inferences about child behaviour.

The psychologists study the child behaviour in order to understand, control and predict future development. Some methods are following:

(1) Biographical method.

(2) Observation method.

(3) Case History method.

(4) Behaviour Rating method.

(5) Checklist and Questionnaire.

(6) Experimental method.

(7) Clinical method.

(8) Differential method.

1. Biographical Method

Biographical method can be used in conjunction with tests and simple experiments. It provide more relevant information and supplement experimental data and observation. Collection of baby biographics is one of the oldest method used in the field of child psychology, the parents as biographer record the information regarding behaviour of child. It is also called baby diary.

2. Observation Method

This method is to observe the child in natural climate of the child. In this, the psychologist is selective and observes a particular type of behaviour in particular situation. The children are observed during force play periods and using a predetermined rating scale of behaviour. Behaviour can be recorded by sound recorder, a motion camera, and one may screen are also used to observe behaviour of children without their knowledge. In this way one get objective information about the child in his natural setting.

3. Case History Method

Case history is a record of all the relevant facts about the child and his environment so that these facts may be seen in proper perspective. It help the child psychologist to help child to lead a happier and productive life. These are the information for conducting a case study:

(a) Physical description of the child.

(b) Family background.

(c) Socio-economic status.

(d) School environment.

(e) Activity of child.

(f) Language.

(g) Motor and cognitive skill.

(h) Interactive with parents, Reeve and teacher.

(i) General behaviour.

(j) Leisure activity.

(k) Frustration.

(l) Early childhood experiences.

(m) Option from different sources.

This is the one common method of assessing children behaviour is case study. It aims at collecting all information about children and environment where they are being up.

Following are the case study approach:

(a) It helps in analyzing the problems of child and solving the problems.

(b) It helps in getting information an any child.

(c) It helps in assessing growth and development of individual.

(d) It helps to identify the bearing style of the child.

(e) It provide records for educator Case studies serves two purposes:

  (i) To gather information and to solve a problem.

  (ii) It makes the subject matter "come alive" a set of coordinated information.

Data for the case study of a child are obtained through interview with the child, his parents, neighbours, relatives, teachers, physician etc.

4. Behaviour Rating

Rating scale is very easy to prepare and use. It takes very little time, i.e., 10-15 minutes, very easy to score and quantity. It is used to study a wide range of behaviours. It requires very little tracing for any one to use it, whether he is a teacher, or parents or any researcher. It can also provide a match between a person's perception and reality.

Rating scales become popular as soon as they are developed. Rating scale identified in five types:

(a) Graphic

(b) Numeric

(c) Standard

(d) Cumulative point

(e) Forced choice

Rating procedure is most simple. The child psychologist observer the behaviour of children for a few days and them assigns ranks i.e., 1st, 2nd, 3rd, 4th etc., as regards creativity, aggressive sociability etc. The rating procedure involves an observer indicating where he believes a child stands on a continuum with respect to some characteristics, trait on type of behaviour. Rating is frequently made on a linear, graphic scale. For example:

Behaviour Rating Scale

1	2	3	4	5	6	7
↓ Very much			↓ Average		↓ Very little	

1. Aggressive ....

2. Fearful ....

3. Social..................................

A sequence of defined numbers is assigned to descriptive categories. The observer select most appropriate number for the behaviour he observes in numerical scale.

In standard rating, the rater is presented with a set of standards against which judgement of others done. This rating procedure is usually done by university.

Format of Standard Rating

Traits	*Top 1%*	*Top 2%*	*Top 5%*	*Top 10%*	*Top 50%*
Intelligence		X		X	
Responsibility			X		

Cumulated joints, rating scale averages men to be rated so that each one acts as a separate indicator of an overall traits. There are negative and positive characteristics i.e. source is positive number negative score, which gives a total picture of trait.

In Forced choice, the rather is given series of descriptive phrases and he is forced to choose one of the alternatives. The child can be best described as: Finally

Cooperative, a good leader, and hard working.

5. Questionnaire and Checklist

Questionnaire which contains a series of verbal questions, widely used an instrument to solicit the opinions and attitudes of children, most useful device in an exploratory study, which measures children's anxiety level, feeling of security etc. A questionnaire with careful administrative and collective of information the technique yield more information in short time. For example:

Q. 1. How many hours does your child?

(a) Play

(b) Sleep

(c) Read

Hence the question elicit the information about the child.

Checklist include in questionnaire method, in this a varies behaviour patterns are mentioned. The child can tick mark in it against all points given in checklist. A checklist is prepared before doing the observation checklist serves four functions:

(a) It is a record of daily activities.

(b) It provides diagnostic information.

(c) It is useful for curriculum planning.

(d) It is very quick.

Checklist call for quantitative judgements about the presence or absence of behaviours.

6. Experimental Method

In experimental method the behaviour of the child is recorded in the most realisable manner and under high degree of control. This is a method of observation under controlled condition. It is primarily used to determine changes in child's behaviour as a result of environmental variables. The technique is most commonly used when the investigator wishes to study a suspected causative relationship holding between a phenomenon of some interest and one or more other factor.

By experimental method, child's behaviour can be reliable observed as compared to other techniques.

7. Clinical Method

Clinical method is very effective method to child when the child displays any problem behaviour of sign are mental tension reflected in his behaviour. During the course of analysing and understanding the child's problems, the clinical psychologist uses data obtained by experimental and differential methods in addition to using his own insight and clinical experiences clinical approach focuses back into the past life to find out what has really made the child to have same problems. As such clinician wants information as is necessary for diagnosing the problem and suggesting remedial measures. It is different from an experimental method. Religious control cannot be used in their method. Insight is more useful.

8. Differential Method

Investigation generally manipulate one variable and arrives at conducting corresponding changes in the dependent child behaviour, in the experimental method. In this method child psychologist compare behaviours with of one group to another group. This method enables one to observe life as it exists and offers greater premise than does and experiments, child psychologist use a combination of methods and techniques in observing children behaviour to make it more meaningful, objectives and comprehensive as well as reliable.

5

Developmental Principles

There is a set of principles that characterizes the pattern and process of growth and development. These principles or characteristics describe typical development as a predictable and orderly process; that is, we can predict how most children will develop and that they will develop at the same rate and at about the same time as other children. Although there are individual differences in children's personalities, activity levels, and timing of developmental milestones, such as ages and stages, the principles and characteristics of development are universal patterns.

Principles of Development

1. **Development Proceeds from the Head Downward:** This is called the cephalocaudle principle. This principle describes the direction of growth and development. According to this principle, the child gains control of the head first, then the arms, and then the legs. Infants develop control of the head and face movements within the first two months after birth. In the next few months, they are able to lift themselves up by using their arms. By 6 to 12 months of age, infants start to gain leg control and may be able to crawl, stand, or walk. Coordination of arms always precedes coordination of legs.

2. **Development Proceeds from the Center of the Body outward:** This is the principle of proximodistal development that also describes the direction of development. This means that the spinal cord develops before outer parts of the body. The child's arms develop before the hands and the hands and feet develop before the fingers and toes. Finger and toe muscles (used in fine motor dexterity) are the last to develop in physical development.

3. **Development Depends on Maturation and Learning:** Maturation refers to the sequential characteristic of biological growth and development. The biological changes occur in sequential order and give children new abilities. Changes in the brain and nervous system account largely for maturation. These changes in the brain and nervous system help children to improve in thinking (cognitive) and motor (physical) skills. Also, children must mature to a certain point before they can progress to new skills (Readiness). For example, a four-month-old cannot use language because the infant's brain has not matured enough to allow the child to talk. By two years old, the brain has developed further and with help from others, the child will have the capacity to say and understand words. Also, a child can't write or draw until he has developed the motor control to hold a pencil or crayon. Maturational patterns are innate, that is, genetically programmed. The child's environment and the learning that occurs as a result of the child's experiences largely determine whether the child will reach optimal development. A stimulating environment and varied experiences allow a child to develop to his or her potential.

4. **Development Proceeds from the Simple (Concrete) to the More Complex:** Children use their cognitive and language skills to reason and

solve problems. For example, learning relationships between things (how things are similar), or classification, is an important ability in cognitive development. The cognitive process of learning how an apple and orange are alike begins with the most simplistic or concrete thought of describing the two. Seeing no relationship, a pre-school child will describe the objects according to some property of the object, such as color. Such a response would be, "An apple is red (or green) and an orange is orange." The first level of thinking about how objects are alike is to give a description or functional relationship (both concrete thoughts) between the two objects. "An apple and orange are round" and "An apple and orange are alike because you eat them" are typical responses of three, four and five year olds. As children develop further in cognitive skills, they are able to understand a higher and more complex relationship between objects and things; that is, that an apple and orange exist in a class called fruit. The child cognitively is then capable of classification.

5. **Growth and Development is a Continuous Process:** As a child develops, he or she adds to the skills already acquired and the new skills become the basis for further achievement and mastery of skills. Most children follow a similar pattern. Also, one stage of development lays the foundation for the next stage of development. For example, in motor development, there is a predictable sequence of developments that occur before walking. The infant lifts and turns the head before he or she can turn over. Infants can move their limbs (arms and legs) before grasping an object. Mastery of climbing stairs involves increasing skills from holding on to walking alone. By the age of four, most children can walk up and down stairs with alternating feet. As in maturation, in order for children to write or draw,

they must have developed the manual (hand) control to hold a pencil and crayon.

6. **Growth and Development Proceed from the General to Specific:** In motor development, the infant will be able to grasp an object with the whole hand before using only the thumb and forefinger. The infant's first motor movements are very generalized, undirected, and reflexive, waving arms or kicking before being able to reach or creep toward an object. Growth occurs from large muscle movements to more refined (smaller) muscle movements.

7. **There are Individual Rates of Growth and Development:** Each child is different and the rates at which individual children grow is different. Although the patterns and sequences for growth and development are usually the same for all children, the rates at which individual children reach developmental stages will be different. Understanding this fact of individual differences in rates of development should cause us to be careful about using and relying on age and stage characteristics to describe or label children. There is a range of ages for any developmental task to take place. This dismisses the notion of the "average child". Some children will walk at ten months while others walk a few months older at eighteen months of age. Some children are more active while others are more passive. This does not mean that the passive child will be less intelligent as an adult. There is no validity to comparing one child's progress with or against another child. Rates of development also are not uniform within an individual child. For example, a child's intellectual development may progress faster than his emotional or social development.

8. **An understanding of the principles** of development helps us to plan appropriate activities and stimulating and enriching experiences for children, and provides a basis for understanding how to encourage and support young children's learning.

Early Experiences

Concept of early experiences involves two things (a) Providing enriched stimulation (b) Accelerating development by compensatory educative.

The concept of early experience can be traced to the writing of Rousseau in the tradition of infant and necessary school in Germany and in the writing of Montessori.

Early experience traditionally been given important roles in intellectual personality, social and emotional development. Early developmental periods are critical because experience occurring during this period have greater impact upon later behaviour and deprivation effects are irreversible.

Early experiences is emphasised because it is during early childhood that engages takes place rapidly, so providing enriched experiences lead to better behavioural change. These experiences vary in terms of language lessons, exposure to new materials, tracing parents for early stimulating but all these programmes have led to significant gains intellectual functioning the gain might be appear due to motivation factors.

The effects of early experiences do not last owner tune unless the programmes are long term on continuous on the natural environment itself is enriching. Hence, gain can be maintained if compensatory educational programmes are introduced to supplement the natural input or environment. Adequate early experience seems to be a necessary but not sufficient condition for later adequate intellectual functioning.

Enriched Environment Means

- Providing children with a chance to the child to explore the environment
- Provide a physically and socially responsive environment
- Provide variety stimulation
- Provide change stimulation to child
- Provide a high level of involvement between child and adult
- Provide adult modelling of desired cognitive skill
- Provide positive reinforces

The effect of early experiences are neither enduring non-irreversible. The evidence are:

(1) Early feeding toilet training and other experiences are not correlated.

(2) Children recover force mild perinatal result, recovery from severe insult in much less likely.

(3) Severely deprived children have shown much of intellectual and social development after much of intervention.

(4) Critical period does not exist, according to various researches.

(5) Brief intervention does not inaculate children against adverse effects.

(6) Maternal deprivation in and of itself does not provide lasting deleterious effects upon children.

Although early experiences is still playing vital role in human development role is not as pervasive as once thought.

Evidence that change in normal development occurs throughout life and that effects of extreme deprivation can be partially countered with intensive therapy should not be misread as implying that plasticity is equivalent across life. Humans are more responsive to many type of experience at a relatively early age.

Early interference with organisation of an organic system is likely to be permanent, whereas interference with the organisation of behaviour through hearing can be overcome through releaving.

Compensatory Education

The rationable that influenced a few of the compensatory education programme approach is the developmental assumption i.e., children earning from weaker section of the community are slow in the rote of development. So for these children education should be given same preschool experience. This approach emphasised that learning experiences are to be provided to children of the weaker section of the community in early childhood since they suffer from environmental deprivation including poverty.

The last approach reinforced by the belief that is possible to ameliorate intellectual deficits. Although Jensen (1969) in his famous article denied the effect of environment an intellectual ability and asserted that compensatory education has been tried and it apparently has failed, a number of well designed compensatory programmes demonstrate remarkable achievement gains. If genetic cultural deficits impair the learning capacity of law SES children, such as children would near be able to learn successfully. This emerin is not tenable in view of the finding from research on compensatory education.

This education programmes are widely in size and scope but they have in common the dual goals of remediation and prevention. They are remedial in the sense that they attempt to full gaps: social, cultural, on academic in the child's total education.

Compensatory programme focus on reading and language development arithmetic, improvement of psychomotor ability, personal and social adjustments. This programmes operated either at preschool years on during the elementary school years and regular school period so that weaker children make up deficiencies before having into the next class. However these programmes do suggest that children coming from weaker section can be helped through enrichment programmes and the degree of their efficiency depends upon how well the programme has been formulated.

In our India, a large segment of children population in the school who come from tribal areas, schedule caste, and facilities who are very poor. These children come to school very rarely under compulsion and very soon dropout from it. Poverty and economic reasons do account for school deep out, yet a great many of their children do not succeed in school because of low ability consequent upon deprivation of come sort on another.

Examining a whole serious of work on the deprived stated that an early enrichment programme at the school level and kindergarden bends may be very helpful in removing the arresting deficits. After all modification in teacher training curriculum, changing the life style characteristics of the deprived, use of accelerated learning programmes and changing the motivational and effective climate of the classroom. Training the deprived children for realistics goal setting, developing self attribution developing a more analytic may of information processing while in school and giving training for intellectual activities and skills where they are deficients. It is essential that parental education is more crucial in so far as providing an enriched interaction environment in early childhood is essential.

Developmental psychologist agree on two basic assumptions:

(a) Environmental factors help determine how fast on slowly children develop intellectual ability.

(b) Experience during the first years of life strongly shape children's relative intellectual functioning condition which remote early childhood development in terms of enriched experience are:

   (i) Favourable interpersonal relationship.

   (ii) Emotional acceptance by parents.

   (iii) Democratic but not permissive family atmosphere.

   (iv) Early role play with increasing confidence.

   (v) Small family structures.

   (vi) Stimulating environment.

Heredity and Environment Interaction

There is also a controversy between the psychologist, biologist, and educationist whether heredity and environment is more important factor for growth and development of an individual. This controversial issue is very significant for the teachers. Heredity is responsible for the growth and development of an individual then the teacher has nothing to do. He has simply to watch how the innate potentiality of the child get unfolded if we consider environment to be responsible for the growth and development of the child, then the role of teacher becomes very important. When he becomes the sole mould the student according to his own ideals. He can shape or pattern the life of the students in the way he likes. Thus he occupies a pivotal place in the process of growth and development. Role of heredity and environment in the process of growth and development from extreme point of view are not at all desirable. those who support heredity to be the only factor responsible growth and development argue that nothing can be done to improve the individual beyond the limits laid down by heredity. Those who support the role of environment to be the most important factor are guilty of exaggerated optimist that there are no limits to the growth and development of an individual.

But it is not possible to have a water tight compartment between the two factors of heredity and development to work for the growth and development of the child. It is not possible to point out the traits in which are exclusively hereditary and environmental. Most of the psychologist are of opinion that the interaction between the energies inherited by an organism and influences of environment are responsible for the growth and development of the individual. It is impossible to say that amount of contribution made by heredity and environment for the growth and development of and individual. Nor is it possible to have water tight compartments between the two factors. From the moment the child is conceived in its mothers womb the two factors worked hard hand-in-hand and continue to pay their roles throughout his life. A study of both the points of view brings us to the conclusions that heredity or environment alone cannot be the sole determinant of the status of an individuals. The combination of two factors in obvious and implicit ways make the individuals what he is.

A child is purely a product of heredity at the times of conception. He receives this heredity from his father and mother, who are having different traits, qualities and characteristics. Each of them contributes to the heredity of the child through genes. A child becomes a distinct individuals with distinct characteristics of his own because of the interaction of genes. Hence the teacher cannot change the influence of heredity on the child. A child who has inherited poor intelligence cannot replace it with superior intelligence by the help of a teacher. Teacher can only help for the development of his intelligence in helping the child with the best use of his intellectual.

Factors Influence in Child Development

1. Heredity and Environment

The influence of heredity on the child begins from the very beginning of life. Soon after conception the organism comes in contact with the environment. The effect of this contact becomes apparent only after birth of a child, who is conceived in a diseased uterus, becomes diseased after birth.

It becomes very easy to understand the influence of environmental set up can easily recognized, because of the marks left on them by the forces operating in the environment in which they live. Being influenced by environment they learn different attitudes, value etc. Malnutrition for a long period and poor hygienic conditions develop certain functional deformities and diseases, which puts a mark in the life of an individual. The teacher plays an important role in moulding the environment of a child. In order to become a successful teacher, he needs to understand the concepts and role of heredity and environment in the life of a child.

2. Maturation and Learning

Maturation is considered as the chief competitor of learning as a modifier of behaviour. Maturation is regarded as those stages of growth and development which takes place from within the subject, without the help any special training, practice experience or stimulation. At a particular stage of development, a child starts crawling, sitting, standing and walking. All these changes in behaviour are the result of maturation. But the ability to talk by a parrot, the ability to drive a motorcycle or to swim in a river, etc. are the product of learning.

Learning sometimes depends upon maturation. A child can learn a thing better, only when reaches a particular maturation level. For example, the age from 1 to 5 years a child can learn the language better, a stimulus response function. All our sense organs are bombarded by the stimuli of the environment and we respond to them. All the sense organs helps us to understand and to interpret the environment to discriminate between good and bad stimulus, to decide to welcome which stimulus and to avoid which one. All these are stages or process of learning activity

Learning to an extent is also a function of maturation. One cannot teach a new born baby to walk or to pick up tiny objects with his fore fingers, however much one may be. Before anything is leant by a person, his sensory motor and also the nervous system including brain must reach a level of maturity. The stages of maturity of the sensory motor and nervous system of an individual. This is called the critical time for that learning. Similarly there is critical time for other important tasks like toilet training, reading, learning behaviors etc. If a child is taught that behaviour before the critical time i.e. before he attained the maturational level for that task, he fails to do so. If he is taught that task after the critical time. He also fails to master it effectively, as is proved from the language problems of the wolf children.

6

Child Care

Introduction

Parents are responsible for the proper up braining of their children. Child rearing calls for a lot of attention, time energy money and commitment that goes with parenthood. The role of mother is very vital in up bringing of her child very often the mother will need the help and support of her husband, parents in-laws and other family members in bringing up the children. The help may also be hired from other sources.

The upbringing of children is a real challenge when both parents are working urbanisation, desire to be independent and breakdown of joint families force the working patents to leave their small infants/children under the care and supervision of parent substitutes.

Needs of Infants and Small Children

The parents look forward to have their own children to Love and to cherish. Having a child at home means that one should be prepared for all basic needs of the baby every child needs to:

- Be-loved and feel physically mentally, and socially secure.

- Have food for optimum growth and development.
- Be clothed for protection against all possible weather conditions. Clothes also contribute to one's personality in any social setup.
- Have a shelter/home that will provide protection against natural calamitics. Shelter also provides the much needed physical security against thieves, burglers and bad elements.
- Sleep soundly, peaceful sleep increases anabolic activities that promote growth among infants and children.
- Be toilet trained in due course. It develops good hygienic habits among children.
- Exercise for the proper tuning up of muscles. Physical fitness is important for each child. A healthy child is capable of having a lot of physical strength that can be learning among children.
- Develop good behaviour needed for proper socialisation. Children learn social values and desirable social behaviour from family school and social environment. Parents and siblings are same of the first role models in the life of a child.
- Have control over their emotions. Small children grow up to be emotional secure and stable when they have a loving and a supportive family.
- Name proper medical care, protection against childhood diseases promotes good health. Each child needs to be immunized to acquire resistance against diseases.
- Be educated, reading, writing and arithmetic are essential in day to day life. Parents provide toys

and baby to books to promote the hearing skills among their loved ones. A home is an essential preparatory schools in the life of each child. The parents should teach the children only when they are ready to learn.

What is Substitute Child Care?

You are now familiar with the needs of small children. These are generally fulfilled by parents in the family. Economic factors often force the mothers to take up jobs. Consequently need to young ones be taken care of by olden siblings, neighbours, or relativeness etc. What role are the siblings, relatives and neighbour playing in bringing up the children? They are mother substitutes while she is at work.

Hence substitute child care can be defined as the care rendered to the child to meet the basic needs in the absence of mother/parent. Substitute care can be made available both at home (siblings, relatives) and outside (creche/day care centres).

Kind of Substitute Child Care

Substitute child care is provided by the following:

(a) Older siblings.

(b) Reatives/neighbours.

(c) Hired help.

(d) Creeche/day care centres.

(e) Vice-nursery/nursery school Balwadi.

Siblings care is very common among families in low income group. Infant and children are left under the care of a slightly older child. You might find a 6 years old child looking after two to three smaller siblings, Slightly older children are not mature enough to care for the young ones. Hence it might be better idea to find an alternative yet safe substitute child care centre.

Relations and Neighbours Can and do play important role in the upbringing of small children in the home itself. Presence of elders in a family with children is a big boom. Grand parents in a family provide very lowing and safe child care. Neighbours can be a family away from your own family. In the absence of suitable mother substitute, neighbours can provide much needed substitute child care. This sort of child care is generally of a short duration.

Hired help is a common features in affluent under families. One should carefully interview the hired help (Ayah/ maid servant) as regards their reliability and experience of being able to provide for all the basic needs of the young one.

Creche: "It is a safe place where small children can be left and looked after while the parents is working". Creche is a day care centre. Parents take their children home after the working houses are over.

Creches take care of children upto 0-3 years of age. Here the children one left under the expert care of qualified and responsible staff/adults. Hence the mothers can carry on with their jobs without anxiety as regards their child.

Specific Needs of Children Upto 0-3 Years

These can be listed as below:

- Feeding the child according to his/her heeds.
- Keeping the child clean.
- Providing facilities for rest and sleep.
- Availability of toys to play with.

- Providing the facility of exercise.
- Clean and safe environment.

Facilities Provided by an Ideal Creche

A creehe should fulfill all the above needs of the small children well organised creches also have the facility of medical check ups for the small children.

(a) Feeding of children very small children are fed by the staff of the creche. All possible care is taken to observe the rules of hygiene while feeding these children.

(i) The milk/food is fed to the child at appropriate time and temperature. Older children are made to wash their hands before and after the meal timings.

(ii) They are made to sit and eat in company. This is how they learn the preliminary table manners.

(b) Keeping the child clean creches will have a certain number of children who as not yet toilet. Hence special care is taken to keep these children clean and dry.

Older children should be encouraged to use toilets to relieve themselves. They should learn to keep toilets clean and also wash their hands with soap and water.

(c) Providing the child with rest and sleeping facilities little children need to sleep and rest while in a comfortable bed. The creche should provide individual cribs for small babies, little children enjoy having their own small pillow and stuffed toy to sleep with.

(d) Toys for playing help the children to socialise in a happy atmosphere. There could be toys to suit the children of different ages, some useful appliances help the child to exercise and explore his/her environment, Walkers, tricycles, small monkey-ladders etc. can be kept in small barricades play area in the creche.

(e) Clean and safe creche environment ensures safety if little children against diseases and accidents. Draine and healthy staffs are the strength of every efficient crehe.

(f) Medical and first air facilities should be available in each creche wherever headed skilled nursing staff could help in emergencies. Availability of a doctor ones in fortnight/month in an added health promotional requirement of a good creche. A first aid kitt should be available at each creche.

Mobile Creches

More than 56 million infants and children in India spend a large part of their waking hours alone, with their parents are busy in fields, in mines, and on construction sites etc.

Mobile creches move along with the workers to the places close to site/mine etc. Mobile creches as important for they provide child care system for labourers.

Mobile creches started about five decades ago to care fox children of construction workers and slum dwellers in Mumbai, Delhi and Pune. Mobile creches information Research centre was set up in January 1991. It undertakes research, documentation publication, and dissemination of expertise and information at national level. More information about mobile creches can be had the following address:

Sector IV,
D12 Area,
Raja Bazar,
Neem Gole
Market
New Delhi

Oxford House
Second floor
Apollo Burder
Mumbai

C/o Scientific
and Research
Centre Progress House
54, Mumbai Pune Road,
Pune

Some large organisations are extending the creche facilities to the children of their own employees only.

Kinder Care

How important it is to find child care you really trust, and a preschool that exceeds your expectations. That's why we're here. Each Kinder Care creates an environment where children are safe, nurtured, loved and encouraged to learn. And at Kinder Care Centers across America, parents are learning why we have become the leading private provider of early childhood education and care in the United States.

Child Care and Educational Opportunities

Kinder Care's recent merger with Knowledge Learning Corporation has created an even more comprehensive system for children and their families across the country. Together we provide high-quality early childhood education and development programmes that focus on the health, safety and development of the whole child.

Kinder Care was founded in 1969 and now operates over 1,250 centers, serving more than 120,000 children between the ages of 6 weeks and 12 years. Knowledge Learning Corporation began as Children's Discovery Centers in 1983 and has since expanded to 740 community centers and more than 450 on-site school programmes. Combined, the companies serve more than 200,000 children, with 1,900 community centers, 656 before-and-after school programmes, and 123 employer-sponsored child care centers in 39 states. Our centers are open throughout the year from Monday through Friday, 6:30 a.m. to 6:00 p.m. (hours may vary by location).

Role of Nursery Schools/Balwadis

Preschool children between the age of 3-5 years go to nursery schools in urban areas. Nursery schools fulfills the basic needs of small children. These schools have an added responsibility of preparing the child for the schooling a ahead. The children fore identified into the learning processes in playway methods. For example, they play and dance to nursery rhymes. Can you recall some of these nursery rhymes you learnt in your childhood?

The privately run nursery schools are relatively more expensive than the usual nursery sections attached to the main schools.

Balwadis provide education to the children in rural areas. They are similar to the nursery schools in towns.

Children learn to draw and paint. They learn to make huge with sand, plasticits/mud. They also learn to identify different shapes and colours.

Nursery schools/balwadis promote the social development in children as they learn to share things and communicable in a social group. The environment in these places helps in the development of language among children. Teachers in these schools often check the hair, nails and clothing of children to make the little ones conscious of personal hygiene and grooming children learn to fantasize and have flights of imagination during such story-feeling sessions. It enhances their mental development.

Integrated Child Development Scheme (ICDS)

Integrated child development scheme was launched in 1975 with the main assumption that a package of multiple services is more effective than providing these facilities one at a time. Initially ICDS was extended to a small population. Today the expansion of ICDS projects has increased considerably as can be seen in the bar chart.

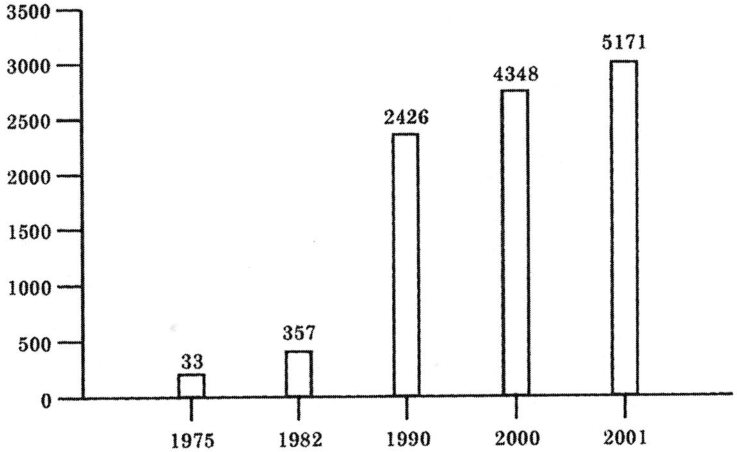

Objectives of ICDS

(a) Improvement of health and nutritional status of children of 0-6 years of age.

(b) Laying foundations for psychological, social and physical development of the child.

(c) Reduction in the incidence of malnutrition, morbidity, mortality and school dropout rates among children.

(d) Effective coordination of the policy and implementation among different departments in order to promote ICDS.

(e) Enhancing capabilities of mothers to look after normal health and nutritional needs of the children.

Target Group

Integrated child development scheme targets at reaching out the package facilities to the following age-groups:

(a) Children 0-6 years of age.

(b) Adolescent girls between 11-18 years.

(c) Women between 15-45 years of age.

(d) All pregnant and lactating women.

Services Rendered by ICDS

It include: (a) Supplement Nutrition. (b) Immunization. (c) Health check ups and referral services, (d) Nutrition and Health education. (e) Non-formal education.

The scheme has successfully reached almost 40 per cent of the deprived children. Double amounts of supplements are given to children below 50-60% of the lowered nutritional standards.

(a) ICDS provides nutritional supplements through the schools and primary health centres. Have you heared of mid-day meals? It is one venue for providing children with cheap. Yet nourishing protein and carbohydrate supplements. Munmura, roasted channa and milk powder are the usual food supplements.

(b) All children should be immunised within the first year against the six killer diseases of early childhood. Can you name these disease studied in the earlier.

(c) The facilities of health checkups and referral services are provided in the Government hospital and municipal dispensaries prenatal and postnatal facilities are provided to mothers and new born babies. The rural as well as the tribal areas are also provided with these medical facilities on regular basis. The medical facilities are fully funded under the government's five years except for the cost of supplements which is borne by the states.

(d) The mothers in the productive years of life are made aware of the importance of spacing, and restricting the size of the family. The relationship between material status and healthy child is highlighted. Mothers with poor maternal status and low weight gain during pregnancy period give birth children weighing less than 2.5 kg (Normal weight at birth for Indian children). Such children remain shorter and higher than their counterparts. They often rate low in the performance throughout life.

ICDS contributes not only to the achievements of women and child goal related to health, nutrition and early child development but also to other primary health care goals and the goals of universal elementary education, as enunciated in the National Plan of Action for Children 1992.

ICDS facilities are provided to the rural population through Anganwadis. All possible efforts are being made to impart formal as well as informal health and nutrition education. Radio, TV, and movies covering these messages to a large section of the population living in urban as well rural areas.

Five Steps to Choosing Quality Child Care

1. Start Early

Start looking as far in advance as you can. No matter what type of care you are considering—a child care center or care in someone else's home—finding the right child care option can take some time.

2. Make a Call

Begin your search by calling your local experts—your child care resource and referral (CCR&R) center. CCR-& R can give you the facts about child care, and a list of child care options in your area that may meet your needs. In addition to what is in this brochure, make sure to ask your CCR&R these things:

- What are the licensing requirements in my area?
- How can I get information about complaints and licensing violations?
- Are there any child care financial assistance programmes that my family qualifies for?

3. Visit and Ask Questions

Make sure you visit the child care options you are considering. Find out about these key indicators of quality:

- **Adult to Child Ratio**: Ask how many children there are for each adult. The fewer the children for each adult, the better for your child. You want your child to get plenty of attention. The younger your child, the more important this is. Babies need an adult to child ratio of no more than 1:4 (one adult for four infants), while four-year-olds can do well with a ratio of 1:10 (one adult for ten children).
- **Group Size**: Find out how many children are in the group. The smaller the group, the better. Imagine a group of 25 two-year olds with five adults, compared to a group of 10 with two adults. Both groups have the same adult to child ratio. Which would be calmer and safer? Which would be more like a family?
- **Caregiver Qualifications**: Ask about the caregivers' training and education. Caregivers with

degrees and/or special training in working with children will be better able to help your child learn. Are the caregivers involved in activities to improve their skills? Do they attend classes and workshops?

- **Turnover:** Check how long caregivers have been at the centre or providing care in their homes. It's best if child stay with the same caregiver at least a year. Caregivers who come and go make it hard on your child. Getting used to new caregivers takes time and energy that could be spent on learning new things.

- **Accreditation**: Find out if the child care provider has been accredited by a national organization. Providers that are accredited have met voluntary standards for child care that are higher than most state licensing requirements. The National Association for the Education of Young Children (NAEYC) and The National Association for Family Child Care (NAFCC) are the two largest organizations that accredit child care programmes.

4. Make a Choice

Think about what you saw at each visit, and make the best choice for your child and family.

5. Stay Involved

The work isn't over when you find good care for your child. You and your child's caregiver are partners now.

Here are some ways to be involved:

- Have parent-caregiver meetings regularly, and ask questions

- Offer to volunteer time when needed, like participating in clean up days, fixing broken toys

- Be there for your child's birthday party
- Visit your child at child care and read a book aloud
- Join in special events, like field trips, Career Day, Black History Month, or other holidays

Even if you can't get time off from work during the day, you can still check in at drop-off and pick-up times. Ask the caregiver how things are going, and how your child is doing.

Visiting and participating in events at your child's provider sends a strong message. It tells your child and your child's caregiver that you think what your child is doing and learning is important.

7

Childhood Diseases

Introduction

In our developing countries nearly a quarter million children die in a week and many millions suffer from poor health and morbidity. Ignorance, as regards the protective of health among children leads to high mortality rate, child is healthy when he/she does not suffer from diseases. Freedom from diseases promotes good health, long life, faithful productive years and economic prosperity of an individual and the nation.

Health and disease differ like day and night as can be seen below:

Health can be defined as the experience of success experienced by an organism in its efforts to respond adaptively to environmental challenges.

Disease defined as the experience of failure experienced by an organism in its efforts to respond adaptively to environmental challenges.

Children Diseases

These diseases occur frequently amongs children. List are given below: Mumps, Diarrhoea, Measles, Cholera, chickenpox, polio, whooping cough, cough and cold, Diptheria, Earache, worm infestation etc.

Diseases are of two main types. They are communicable and non-communicable diseases. Communicable diseases spread rapidly through the medium of dust, air, food, water, contact, insects bites and agents.

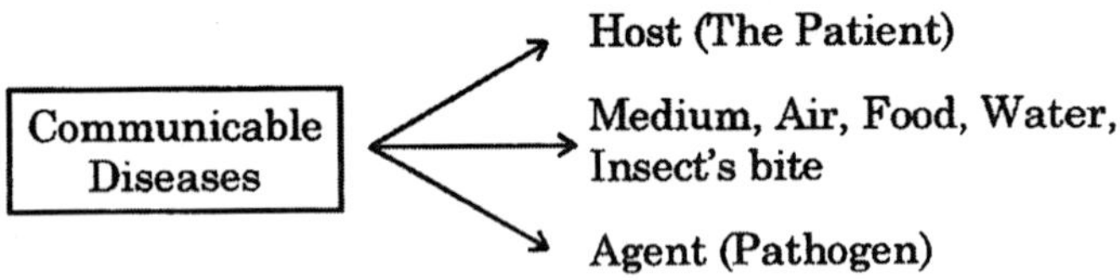

Agents (pathogens include micro-organism like bacteria, virus and worms.

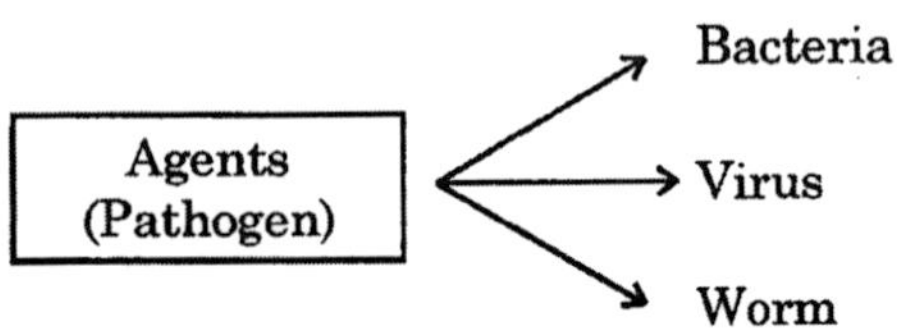

Communicable disease means it spreads from one person to another.

Non-communicable disease means it does not spread from one person to another.

Prevention and Control of Communicable Diseases

Communicable diseases can be prevented and controlled by the following three factors.

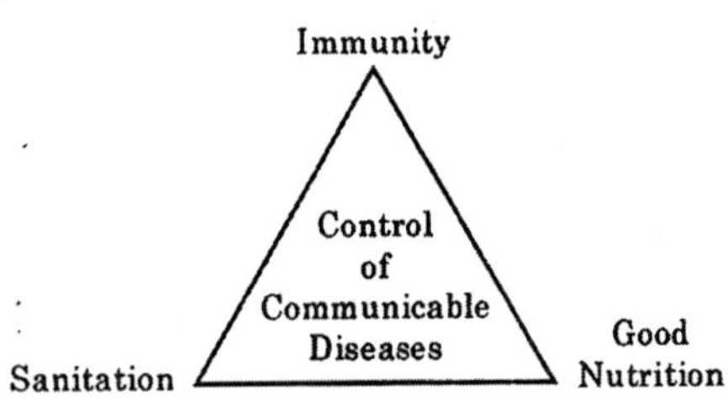

Children's Diseases and Control Measures

Medium of disease spread	*Childhood diseases*	*Control measures*
Air get polluted by patient's cough, sneeze, with covering nose and mouth.	Influenza, tuberclosis, whooping cough, measles, chickenpox, mumps.	(i) Mouth and nose should be covered. (ii) Paper tissue used to clean. (iii) Sanitary disposal of tissues is essential.
Water and food polluted by unhygenic condition of cooking, storing of food, eating, low level of personal hygiene, use dirty vessels, food exposed to floors and direct consumption of unsafe water.	Diarrhoea, dysentery, cholera, jaundice, polio etc.	(i) Boiled water. (ii) Keep food covered. (iii) Avoid licking food. (iv) Avoid put directly fingers in food. (v) Wash hand before serving foods.
Insect Bite—Causing germs, gets transferred from sick person to a healthy person.	Malaria, filaria, viral fever	(i) Keep environment clean. (ii) Protect house by using wire mesh. (iii) Use long sleeves dress. (iv) Sleep under mosquito nets.
Soil polluted by wastes are not properly disposed of.	Tetanus, worms.	(i) Have proper footwear. (ii) Clean wound properly. (iii) Do not pick up foods from dirts.
Disease spread by directly and indirectly by contacts.	Scabies, Eczema, Diphtheria, Skin diseases.	(i) Avoid contact with sick persons. (ii) Do not use sick's children toy. (iii) Do not use clothes of sick.

Importance of personal hygiene and sanitation has also been formally studied in your health classes.

Barriers Against Disease Germs

Body resists the entry of disease germs and after resistance in many ways.

Barriers of Body

(i) **Skin:** The germ cannot find entry unless the skin in damaged. Mucin secreted by mucous membranes repel bacteria.

(ii) **Saliva:** The antiseptic qualities of the saliva are well known. The germ can also be expelled from the body by coughing out.

(iii) **Tear Glands:** Produce secretion containing lysozyme which has a potential of killing and washing away the germs.

(iv) **Nasal:** Opening have cillia that sweep out the germs to some extent. Sneezing can expel bacteria.

(v) **Urine and Facees:** Besides excreting body waste, also gets rid of some of the pathogens.

(vi) **Stomach:** Secrets "pepsin hydrochloric acid" that burns away some of the germs. The stomach has the unique ability of rejecting its contents if one has consumed highly contaminated food.

(vii) **Blood:** Contains white blood cells. The WBCs more like the single cell amoeba. They engulf the bacteria and release a ferment to liquefy bacteria.

(viii) **Lymph Nodes:** These nodes engulf the disease germs and kill them. The lymph nodes may become enlarged and painful due to excessive infection.

Definition of Immunity

Immunity can be defined as the ability of an individual to resist disease and death.

How Immunity Developed ?

Micro-organisms and the pathogens are recognised as enemies. They contain antigens that stimulate. The production of antibodies to build up body defence mechanism. The body needs to produce different antibodies for providing protection against the various disease germs.

Types of Immunity

Immunity are two types, i.e., Natural and Acquired. Acquired immunity can be naturally or artificiálly induced.

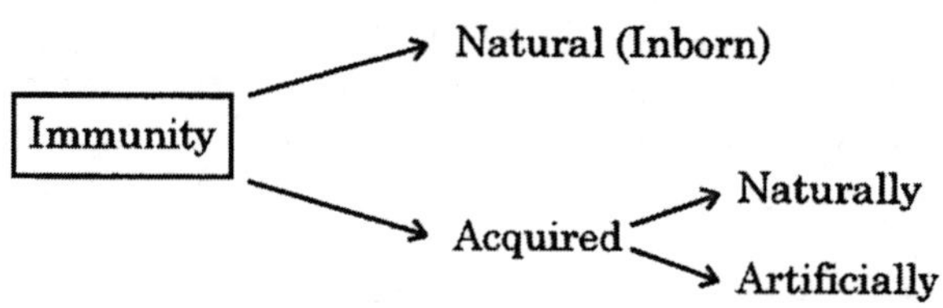

Natural immunity is present at birth. Some antibodies also get transferred from mother to the infant during breast feeding. Hence breast feeding of infants is very important.

Childhood Diseases Preventable by Immunization

Disease against which the children can be immunised?

Tuberculosis, peretusive, polio diptheria, mumps, whooping cough tetanus, measles, hepatitis.

Immunization can be defined as the process of developing immune bodies antibodies in an individual by artificially introducing controlled number of germs into the body. This stimulates the production of antibodies and provides immunity against diseases.

Immunity and Advantages of Breast Feeding

The most appropriate baby food is the mother's milk. The mother's milk has all the nutrients needed by the baby in just right proportions. This milk is safe, sterile and contains antibodies which provide immunity against diseases. The initial milk has colostrum, thick yellowish milky secretion, that has a high antibody content. It should be definitely fed to the child to provide natural immunity.

Babies who are breast fed have lesser ailments and have better nutritional status. Bottle feeding with deluted milk formula and insanitary conditions among the poor cause diarrhoea and other gastro intestinal problems resulting in malnutrition. Frequent sucking stimulates the production of milk. Feeding the baby is satisfying both mother and child.

Breast fed babies are emotionally secure and physically healthy. Every mother has potential for meeting the milk requirement of her baby. As the child grows the breast feeds could be supplemented with easy to digest, self and liquidity meaning foods.

Naturally acquired immunity is achieved by actually having the disease. The body of the child will produce its own antibodies to fight the germs. The child has to be strong to withstand the pain and suffering caused by the disease germs. The naturally acquired immunity is also known as actively acquired immunity.

In the case of artificially acquired immunity the weakened on dead germs are introduced into the body and the body is stimulated to produce its own antibodies without actually having the disease. This is less painful than the naturally acquired immunity.

Immunization Schedule

BCG (Bacillus Calmelte Guerin)

It is named after the French bacteriologists Calmetle and Guerin. It provides protectitly against tuberculosis. The

Protect from Childhood Diseases

	Tuberculosis	*Diptheria*	*Pertussis*	*Tetanus*
Mode of spread	Air	Air and direct contact with sick child and disease carriers	Air	Dirty soil rusted metal parts.
Causative agent	Tubercular Bacillus bacteria	Bacteria	Pertusis coming out with cough	Tetanus bacillus, bacteria
Age of occurrence	Children of all ages	upto 5 yrs.	upto 5 yrs.	Children of all ages
Incubation period	4-6 weeks	2-5 days	1-2 weeks	4-14 days.
Symptoms	(1) Weakness (2) Less weight (3) Less appetite (4) Rapid pulse (5) Low grade fever (6) Foul breath (7) Cough.	(1) High fever (2) Sore throat (3) Swelling of tonsil (4) Swallowing difficulty. (5) Paralysis of eye abdomen arms, legs	(1) Severe cough (2) (3) Whooping (4) Vomiting (5) Tired feeling	(1) Fever (2) Headache (3) Restlessness (4) Difficulty in chewing (5) Locking jar (6) Back bend
Season	Any season	Cold months	Jan-Mar.	Any season

(Contd.)

(Contd. Table)

	Tuberculosis	*Diptheria*	*Pertussis*	*Tetanus*
Duration of Disease	Long term care	Few days	Few weeks	Few weeks
Care of Disease	(1) Isolated the child (2) Keep the patient in clean room (3) Healthy food care (4) Doctor's supervision	(1) Do not give infected toys (2) Isolated (3) Early diagonosis (4) Doctor's care	(1) Keep child warm (2) Avoid play (3) Doctor's care	(1) Doctor's care (2) Keep cotton between teeth (3) Avoid tongue bites.
Prevention	BCG vaccine	DTP vaccine	DPT vaccine	DPT vaccine

vaccine injected with the dermis on the left side. It is given at birth as soon after local reaction may occur 3-4 weeks later.

DPT (Diphtheria, Pentussis, Tetanus)

It is a tripple vaccine providing immunity against diphtheria, pertusis (whooping cough) and tetanus. The first dose is injected at the age of 6 weaks of age the subsequent two dose are given at an interval of 4 weaks.

DTaP is the updated version of DPT. The 'a' stands for "accellular" as only a part of the pertusis bacteria is used in the vaccine.

Polio: It is an oral vaccine providing immunity against attack of the crippling polio disease. It is now available in oral form and is given three doses starting at birth. The second and third doses are given at an interval of 4-8 weeks each. Additional polio vaccine doses are given to children to eradicate this disease.

MMR (Measles, Mumps and Rubella)

It is the latest vaccine providing immunity for three disease. It is given in a single dose in an injectable form at the age of 9 months. It provides immunity again mumps, measles and rubella.

Typhoid: It is a food and water borne disease caused by bacillus bacteria. The disease is characterised by fever and malice. The available heat phenol inactivated typhoid vaccine provides limited protection only. It is an injectable vaccine and can be given at 2 years of age second dose can be repeated an interval of 3-6 weeks.

Hepatitis B Vaccine: It provides protection against a virus that causes inflamation of liver resulting in Jaundice. The virus is transmitted through contaminated needles and 0blood transfusion. New born babies are likely to get it form carrier mother. It is a serious disease. First dose can be given at birth, second after 1-2 months and third 6-18 months.

	Polio	*Measles*	*Mumps*	*Rubella*
Mode of spread	Food of water	Infected nose, throat secretion passed on as drop lets.	Direct close contact, infe-cted through saliva of soil	Spread by direct contact
Causative agent	Virus	Virus	Virus	Virus
Age of occurence	Affects young children	Ten months to eight years	Occurs in children of adolescent	Attacks children 3-12 yrs.
Incubation period	7-12 days Upto 21 days	10-12 days	12-26 days	12-15 days
Season	Hot weather	Jan-April	Any season	Any season
Duration of disease	15 days	11-12 days	7-10 days	8-12 days
Care of patient	Give sufficient water Doctor's instruction	Isolate the child Deamlight provide avoid play.	Isolate the patient Give liquid food Gargle the mouth	Soft meal Isolate the patient Doctor's opinion follow

(Contd.)

(Contd. Table)

	Polio	*Measles*	*Mumps*	*Rubella*
Symptoms	(1) General ill health. (2) Fever about 100°F (3) Headache and derasy (4) Vomitting, pain (5) Tenderness (6) Paralysis	(1) Cough and running nose (2) Fever with chills (3) Rashes appear (4) Some eyes (5) Iching and irritative	(1) Fever (2) Enlargement of salivary gland (3) Smelling at base of ears (4) Earaches. (5) Dry mouth (6) Damage brain and spinal cord	(1) Cold (2) Cough. (3) Rashes
Prevention	Polio vaccine in 3 doses	MMR vaccine	MMR vaccine	MMR vaccine

(i) All vaccines should be give to protect the child and a proper record of these shots should be kept.

(ii) Booster doses of DPT and polio are given between 16-24 months. These are repeated when the child joins school. Tetanus is short lived. The tetanus shot needs to be repeated as and when the child gets an oped wound with rusted and dirty objects.

(iii) Under the National Immunization Programme the children are also being given prophylactic doses of oreal vitamin A to provide protection against blindness.

Chickenpox: Their disease is common among children and is caused by a virus. The incubation period spans 14-21 days. It is an air borne infection and spreads by direct and indirect contact. Coughing and sneezing by sick child release large numbег of germs. Sick has fever and headache. Rashes appear all ver the body and Rashes fill with to form blisters and caus s uncomfortable iching. Application of calamine lotion relieves iching. The rash dries to form scabs that are infectiens. There is possibility of respiratory problems like pneumonia. The disease lasts for about 21 days.

Cholera: It is caused by bacillus bacteria called "vibrio-coma". It spreads fast with the consumption of infected food and water. The incubation period is short, i.e., 1-5 days. The disease characterised by loose watery motions that look like "rice water". It is accompanied by vomitting resulting in extreme fluid and electrolyte loss. The patient gets cramp and feels extremely thirsty. Suppression of urine leads to the accumulation of toxic materials in the body. The child should be given plenty of fluids to avoid dehydration.

Diarrhoea: It is a condition where the stomach becomes loose due to infection. The infections agents and parasites (worms) enter the system due to poor environmental sanitation and low standard of personal hygiene.

Revised Immunization Chart for Small Children

Name of Child .... Parent's Name ....

Ph. No. .... Dob ....

Age	*Immunization*	*Disease*	*Form of Admin*	*Dose*
Birth	Polio,	Polio,	Oral	1st dose
	hepatis	jaundice	injection	1st dose
1st month	BCG, polio	tuberculosis	injection	Single dose
	Hepatis-B	polio	Oral	2nd dose
		jaundice	injection	2nd dose
2nd month	DTP	Diptheria	injection	1st dose
	Polio	Pertusis	oral	3rd dose
		Tetanus		
		polio		
3rd month	DTP	Diptheria	injection	3rd dose
	Polio	Pertusis	oral	4th dose
		Tetanus		
		Polio		
4th month	DTP	Diptheria	injection	3rd dose
	Polio	Pertusis	oral	5th dose
		Tetanus		
		Polio		

Contd.

Contd.

Age	*Immunization*	*Disease*	*Form of Admin*	*Dose*
6th month	Hepatitis-B	Jaundice	Injection	3rd dose
9th month	Measles vaccine	Measles	Injection	1st dose
12th month	Vit-A	Blindness	Oral	Prophylactic dose
15th month	MMR	Measles Mumps Rubella	Injection	Single dose
18th month	DPT Polio	Diphtheria Pertussis Tetanus Polio	Injection Oral	1st booster dose 1st booster dose
24th month	Typhoid shot	Injection	Single dose	Single dose
48th month	DPT polio	Diphtheria Pertusis Tetanus Polio	Injection Oral	2nd booster dose 2nd booster dose

Frequently watery stools may be accompanied by stomachache. The child feels week and thirsty. Ignorant mothers try to control diarrhoea by restricting the fluid intake. The child suffers dehydration which if uncontrolled could prove fatal. Skin looses its elasticity and it controlled local rehydration solution by ORS.

Dysentery: It is caused by Entamoeba histolytica and bacillus bacteria. The incubation period is short and the child an recover within a week. The child will have "gripping" stomach pain and pass frequent stoks. Sometimes the stools may be accompanied by traces of mucous and blood. This results in general weakness. The course of treatment and control is similar as in diarrhoea.

Influenza and Common Cold: These are minor ailments causing considerable discomfort among little babies. Influenza is caused by a virus. The incubation period is very short and the disease spreads though air as well as close contact. It is characterised by cough, running nose, sneezing and fever. It is a good practice to cover your nose/mouth while sneezing.

The child should be protected from air draughts and isolated from siblings and other children. Warm milk, soups and vegetables broths and egg-nog etc. can be given to the child build up strength to fight the disease germs. It is a good practice to cover your mouth/nose while sneezing.

Ear Infections: Accompany cough, cold influenza and other respiratory problems. The discharge and wax accumulate in the care and cause terrible pain to the child. The child may also have fever at times immediate treatment provides relief and safety against possible hearing impairment.

Sore Eyes: These eyes are quite common among children living in slums and poor sanitary conditions. The eyes become sticky, cause itching and have burning sensations. The eyelids get swollen. It is highly communicable conditions. Eyes could be mashed and given hot formentation with luke warm saline water.

Scabies: The baby skin is soft and tender poor personal and environmental sanitation results in scabies that is caused by itchvite. The itching spread fast. The scabies can be controlled by bathing the child with antiseptic and genetic soap. The personal clothing and bedding of all family members needs to be cleaned and sunned.

Boils: Boils in baby skin have pus-forming staphylococcus bacteria. The boils are inflamed and painful. Clean the boils with worm saline water and apply antiseptic cream as advised by the doctor.

Thread Worm Infection : In female the worm is 8-13 mm long and the male worm is half the size. The worms attach themselves to the folds of skin around anus. These can be seen with naked eye at the anus and cause a lot of itching. The itching fingers and nails pickup the eggs laid by the female worm and find entry into the mouth. The eggs turn into larva into the duodenum and pass down to the large intestine and out to anus as worm. These worms cause loss of appetite, restlessness, cough, sleepiness, and even convulsion. The nails should be trained and the hands kept clean. Son child's napkins, bed clothes and towels to sleep with their siblings till cured, clean the child's anus thoroughly after the child has passed the stools. Smear anus with ammoniated mercury ointment.

Protection and Prevention Childhood Diseases

Protect Your Child

We have record or near record low levels of vaccine-preventable childhood diseases in the United States, but that does not mean these have disappeared. Many of the viruses and bacteria are still circulating in this country or are only a plane ride away. That's why it's important that children, especially infants and young children, receive recommended immunizations on time.

Childhood Vaccination Schedule

Childhood Vaccination Schedule which indicates the recommended ages for routine administration of the currently licensed childhood vaccines for children through 18 years of age. This schedule has been approved by the Advisory Committee on Immunization Practices (ACIP), the American Academy of Pediatrics (AAP), and the American Academy of Family Physicians (AAFP).

Descriptions of Vaccine-Preventable Diseases

The following vaccine-preventable diseases, not long ago, disabled and killed millions of American children. Thanks to our country's high childhood immunization coverage levels, these diseases are now very uncommon.

- Diphtheria
- Haemophilus influenzae type b (Hib)
- Hepatitis A
- Hepatitis B
- Measles
- Mumps
- Pertussis (whooping cough)
- Pneumococcal disease
- Polio
- Rubella (German measles)

- Tetanus (lockjaw)
- Varicella (chickenpox)

Diphtheria

Description	A respiratory disease caused by bacteria.
Symptoms	Gradual onset of a sore throat and low-grade fever.
Complications	Airway obstruction, coma, and death if not treated.
Transmission	Spread by coughing and sneezing.
Vaccine	Diphtheria toxoid (contained in DTP, DTaP, DT or Td vaccines) can prevent this disease.

Haemophilus Influenzae Type b (Hib)

Description	A severe bacterial infection, occurring primarily in infants.
Symptoms	Skin and throat infections, meningitis, pneumonia, sepsis, and arthritis. (Can be serious in children under age 1, but there is little risk of getting the disease after age 5)
Complications	Hib meningitis (death in one out of 20 children, and permanent brain damage in 10%-30% of the survivors)
Transmission	Spread by coughing and sneezing.
Vaccine	Hib vaccine can prevent this disease.

Hepatitis A

Description	A disease of the liver caused by hepatitis A virus.
Symptoms	Potentially none (likelihood of symptoms increases with the person's age). If present: yellow skin or eyes, tiredness, stomach ache, loss of appetite, or nausea.
Complications	Because young children might not have symptoms, the disease is often not recognized until the child's caregiver becomes ill with hepatitis A.
Transmission	*Most often:* Spread by the fecal-oral route (An object contaminated with the stool of a person with hepatitis A is put into another person's mouth.) *Less often:* Spread by swallowing food or water that contains the virus
Vaccine	Hepatitis A vaccine will prevent this disease.

Hepatitis B

Description	A disease of the liver caused by hepatitis B virus.
Symptoms	Potentially none when first infected (likelihood of early symptoms increases with the person's age). *If present:* Yellow skin or eyes, tiredness, stomach ache, loss of appetite, nausea, or joint pain.

Complications	The younger the person, the greater the likelihood of staying infected and having life-long liver problems, such as scarring of the liver and liver cancer.
Transmission	Spread through contact with the blood of an infected person or by having sex with an infected person.
Vaccine	Hepatitis B vaccine is will prevent this disease.

Measles

Description	A respiratory disease caused by a virus.
Symptoms	Measles virus causes rash, high fever, cough, runny nose, and red, watery eyes, lasting about a week.
Complications	Diarrhea, ear infections, pneumonia, encephalitis, seizures, and death.
Transmission	Spread by coughing and sneezing (highly contagious).
Vaccine	Measles vaccine (contained in MMR, MR and measles vaccines) can prevent this disease.

Mumps

Description	A disease of the lymph nodes caused by a virus.
Symptoms	Fever, headache, muscle ache, and swelling of the lymph nodes close to the jaw.

Complications	Meningitis, inflammation of the testicles or ovaries, inflammation of the pancreas and deafness (usually permanent).
Transmission	Spread by coughing and sneezing
Vaccine	Mumps vaccine (contained in MMR) can prevent this disease.

Pertussis (Whooping Cough)

Description	A respiratory disease caused by bacteria.
Symptoms	Severe spasms of coughing that can interfere with eating, drinking, and breathing.
Complications	Pneumonia, encephalitis (due to lack of oxygen), and death, especially in infants.
Transmission	Spread by coughing and sneezing (highly contagious).
Vaccine	Pertussis vaccine (contained in DTP and DTaP) can prevent this disease.

Pneumococcal Disease

Description	A type of bacteria:
Symptoms	Pneumococcal pneumonia (begins with high fever, cough, and stabbing chest pains), bacteremia, and meningitis.
Complications	Death (one of the most common causes of death in America from a vaccine-preventable disease).

Transmission	Pneumococcus is in many people's noses and throats. Why it suddenly invades the body and causes disease is unknown.
Vaccine	Pneumococcal Conjugate Vaccine (PCV especially developed for infants and children under age 2) and Pneumococcal Polysaccharide Vaccine (PPV not effective for children under 2 years—only for adults) can prevent this disease.

Polio

Description	A disease of the lymphatic and nervous systems.
Symptoms	Fever, sore throat, nausea, headaches, stomach aches, and stiffness in the neck, back, and legs.
Complications	Paralysis that can lead to permanent disability and death.
Transmission	Contact with an infected person
Vaccine	Polio vaccine (IPV) can prevent this disease.

Rubella (German Measles)

Description	A respiratory disease caused by a virus.
Symptoms	Rash and fever for two to three days (mild disease in children and young adults)
Complications	Birth defects if acquired by a pregnant woman: deafness, cataracts, heart

	defects, mental retardation, and liver and spleen damage (at least a 20% chance of damage to the fetus if a woman is infected early in pregnancy).
Transmission	Spread by coughing and sneezing.
Vaccine	Rubella vaccine (contained in MMR vaccine) can prevent this disease.

Tetanus (Lockjaw)

Description	A disease of the nervous system caused by a bacteria
Symptoms	*Early symptoms:* Lockjaw, stiffness in the neck and abdomen, and difficulty swallowing. Later symptoms: *fever, elevated blood pressure, and severe muscle spasms.*
Complications	Death in one third of the cases, especially people over age 50.
Transmission	Enters the body through a break in the skin.
Vaccine	Tetanus toxoid (contained in DTP, DT, DTaP and Td vaccines) can prevent this disease.

Varicella (Chickenpox)

Description	A virus of the herpes family
Symptoms	A skin rash of blister-like lesions, usually on the face, scalp, or trunk
Complications	Bacterial infection of the skin, swelling of the brain, and pneumonia (usually

	more severe in children 13 or older and adults)
Transmission	Spread by coughing and sneezing (highly contagious)
Vaccine	Varicella vaccine can prevent this disease.

Chickenpox

Symptoms

Red, quite itchy, spots or blisters are scattered over the entire body and the child has a moderate fever.

Treatment

Symptomatic treatment with calamine lotion to reduce itching. Antiviral medicine in severe cases.

Incubation Period

Between 10 to 20 days from being exposed to the infection and showing symptoms.

Infectious Period

Chickenpox is contagious before the disease breaks out and may be so until the last spots have disappeared and the scabs or crusts have fallen off. The child should stay home until the crusts have fallen off and the blisters are no longer weeping.

Erythema Infectiosum

Symptoms

The child has red specks on the cheeks, nose, arms, thighs and buttocks. These are often blurred which makes it look like the child has been slapped. This disease often known as 'slapped cheek' syndrome. It can last up to 14 days and rarely causes a fever. It is mostly seen in children between the ages of 4 and 12.

Treatment

It cannot be treated, but disappears by itself. It is usually quite a mild illness.

Incubation Period

Two weeks between being exposed to the infection and showing symptoms.

Infectious Period

Once the rash appears, the disease is no longer infectious.

Complications

Pregnant women should avoid being in contact with children with fifth disease as it may cause a miscarriage. Pregnant women with a child who contracts fifth disease should contact their doctor. The incubation period is a couple of weeks.

Three-day-fever (Roseola Infantum)

Symptoms

A child with three-day-fever has a high fever for three days and a pink rash covers their body. It is mostly seen in children under the age of three years.

Treatment

Undress the child to ensure they aren't too warm. Give the child fever reducing medication (e.g. paracetamol) to control their temperature and plenty of fluids to avoid dehydration.

Incubation Period

Between 10 to 15 days from being exposed to the infection and showing symptoms.

Infectiousness

It is contagious during the whole period of the disease and up to two to three days after. Avoid contact with other children under three years of age during the whole period.

Hand, Foot and Mouth Disease

Symptoms

The child has a large number of small spots and blisters, particularly in the mouth and on the feet and hands. The disease can cause a slight fever for a few days.

Treatment

As with most diseases causing a fever, it is important to make sure the child gets plenty to drink. If the ulcers in their mouth are severe it may help to mash up the child's food.

Incubation Period

Two to three days between being exposed to the infection and showing symptoms.

Infectious Period

The disease is contagious as long as blisters or spots are still present.

Scarlet Fever

Symptoms

The child has a slight to moderate fever, a sore throat and a rash which is often located in their armpits or groin. The child's skin peels and they get a coarse, pink tongue-a condition known as strawberry tongue.

Treatment

Antibiotics are usually given for this disease. It is important to keep the child at home and avoid contact with other children.

Incubation Period

Three to eight days between being exposed to the infection and showing symptoms.

Childhood Immunization

At the beginning of the 20th century, infectious diseases were widespread in the United States and there were few effective treatments. Many thousands of people died from smallpox, measles, diphtheria, and pertussis. Since 1900, many vaccines have been developed to control infectious diseases. The Centers for Disease Control (CDC) has reported dramatic declines in deaths for the nine vaccine-preventable diseases for which vaccination has been universally recommended for children. Smallpox was eradicated in 1977; consequently, vaccination for this disease no longer is necessary. As of 1991, polio caused by wild-type viruses has been eliminated from the Western Hemisphere. Measles and Haemophilus influenzae type b among children less than five years old have been reduced to record low numbers of cases.

Since the federal government promoted the use of polio vaccination after the vaccine was introduced in 1955, federal, state, and local governments and public and private health-care providers have worked together to develop and maintain the vaccine-delivery system.

What are Immunizations?

Immunity is when antibodies fight infectious diseases and stay in your system, even after the disease is gone, to protect you from getting sick again. Newborn babies have natural immunity to many diseases because they have antibodies they got from their mothers, but this immunity wears off before the baby's first birthday. Even after the natural immunity wears off, children can be protected against many diseases by vaccinating them against those diseases.

How Vaccines Work

Vaccines contain weak or dead disease germs. After the vaccine is given, either by injection or in a liquid form that is swallowed, the body makes antibodies to fight the weak or dead germs in the vaccine just as it would react to the disease itself. These antibodies remain in the child's body to safeguard the child from the real disease germs if they invade the child's body.

The Safety of Vaccinations

Vaccines, like all medications, can have some negative side effects. Most of the effects are mild, such as rash, soreness at the site of injection, or a mild fever. Serious reactions to vaccines are extremely rare, but do occur. For most children, however, the risk of contracting the disease is far greater than the risk of a serious reaction to the vaccination.

Why Immunizations are Important?

Vaccines are one of the greatest achievements of medical science and public health. But in spite of the dramatic declines in vaccine-preventable diseases, such diseases still exist, particularly in developing countries. Children need immunizations to keep them healthy and to protect them from dangerous childhood diseases. Without vaccines, epidemics of vaccine-preventable diseases would return, resulting in increased illness, disability, and death.

Unfortunately some children and adults do not get all of their necessary vaccinations. This is caused by fear, religious or personal beliefs, lack of access to health care, or a lack of understanding. There also are many misconceptions about vaccines that keep people from being properly protected. Immunizations for childhood diseases are now required by law in all states, and children may not be allowed to attend day care or school or participate in sports activities if they have not been immunized.

Childhood Diseases Prevented by Vaccines

The following is a summary from the Centers for Disease Control of the childhood diseases for which children routinely are immunized:

Diphtheria is a throat and respiratory infection spread by coughing and sneezing. It initially causes a sore throat and mild fever. It can lead to breathing problems, paralysis, heart failure, and even death.

Haemophilus influenzae type b (Hib) is a serious bacterial infection that can cause meningitis, sepsis, cellulitis, pneumonia, brain damage, infections, and death. It is most common in children less than five years of age. Before Hib immunizations became available, Hib was the most common cause of bacterial meningitis among infants and children in the United States. According to the CDC, the incidence of Hib has declined by 97 to 99 per cent since Hib vaccine was introduced in 1987.

Hepatitis B is caused by a virus that attacks the liver. The virus causes jaundice, fatigue, abdominal pain, loss of appetite, intermittent nausea, and vomiting. It can result in lifelong infection, cirrhosis of the liver, liver cancer, liver failure, and death.

Measles is a highly contagious disease that causes rash, fever, and coughing. It can lead to ear infections, diarrhea, pneumonia, seizures, brain damage, and death. The measles virus is common throughout the world and is frequently imported into the United States. The CDC estimates that as many as 1 of every 1,000 persons with measles will die.

Mumps causes fever, headache and swelling of one or both cheeks or sides of the jaw. It can lead to hearing loss and meningitis. Adult males who contract mumps may experience painful, swollen testicles.

Rubella (German measles) is usually a mild disease in children and adults that causes rash, swollen glands, and fever. However, it causes severe birth defects (including heart disease, blindness, deafness, and brain damage) if acquired by a pregnant woman. In 1964-1965, before rubella immunization was routine in the United States, an epidemic of rubella resulted in an estimated 20,000 infants born with birth defects, with 2,100 neonatal deaths and 11,250 miscarriages.

Polio causes acute paralysis that can lead to permanent physical disability or death. Before polio vaccine was available, annual epidemics of polio often left thousands of victims (mostly children) in braces, crutches, wheelchairs, and iron lungs. Polio vaccines and polio immunization programmes have eliminated polio caused by wild polio viruses in the entire Western Hemisphere.

Pertussis (Whooping cough) is a highly contagious respiratory disease. Pertussis can cause prolonged coughing spells that can last for weeks. These spells can make it difficult for a child to eat, drink, and breathe. It can lead to pneumonia, seizures, brain damage, and death. In the United States, most cases of pertussis are in children less than five years old, and half of those are in infants less than one year old. Before pertussis immunizations were available in the United States, between 150,000 and 260,000 cases of pertussis were reported each year, with up to 9,000 pertussis-related deaths.

Rotavirus is the most common cause of severe diarrhea among children. It also causes vomiting, fever, and abdominal pain. It results in the death of over 600,000 children annually worldwide. In 1998, rotavirus vaccine was approved for use in the United States for children less than six months of age. The vaccine does not completely protect against infection but it prevents severe disease from occurring in about 70-80 per cent of children who take it.

Tetanus (lockjaw) is a disease that enters the body through a break in the skin and then produces a toxin that attacks the nervous system. It causes severe muscle spasms, usually all over the body. A person's jaw can become "locked" so the person cannot open his or her mouth or swallow. Tetanus can lead to death. In the United States, most cases are in adults, but in developing countries, tetanus frequently affects newborn babies. More than 500,000 babies died from tetanus in 1993.

Varicella (chickenpox) is a highly contagious virus that causes a skin rash, usually on the face, scalp, or trunk. It usually is more severe in older children and adults. Complications are rare. Children who contract this disease are quarantined from school.

Immunizations Children should Receive

DTP vaccine protects children against diphtheria, tetanus, and pertussis. A newer version of the vaccine is called DTaP. The vaccine is a five-shot series that typically is completed by the time a child is six years old.

Td is a booster shot for diphtheria and tetanus. It typically is given at age 11 to 12 years and then every 10 years through adulthood.

Hib vaccine inoculates children against Haemophilus influenzae type b. The Hib vaccine is a series of three or four shots typically completed by age 15 months.

Polio vaccine is either oral (OPV) or injected (IPV). It is given in four doses that are usually completed by the time a child starts kindergarten.

HBV is the hepatitis B vaccine. The first dose of this vaccine routinely is given to all infants and the two additional does are given by 18 months.

MMR is the measles-mumps-rubella vaccine. It is a two-shot series, with the first dose given by 15 months of age and the second by the time a child starts kindergarten.

Varicella (chickenpox) vaccine is relatively new and typically is given between 12 and 18 months and to adults who did not have chickenpox as children.

When Immunizations should be Given?

Immunizations must begin at birth and most vaccinations should be completed by age two. By immunizing by age two, children are protected from being infected and from infecting others at school or at daycare centers.

A vaccination health record is important to help parents and their health care provider keep the child on schedule. A record should be started at birth when the child receives his or her first vaccination and updated each time the child receives the next scheduled vaccination. This information will help parents if they move to a new area or change health care providers, or when their child enrolls in daycare or starts school.

Summary

- Health refers to the experiences of success in facing the challenges of day to day life. Disease is the failure to do so.
- Every communicable disease has three components viz., agent, medium and the host.
- Body barriers resist the entry of disease germs.
- Immunity is the ability to resist disease.

- Immunization can prevent TB, diphtheria, pertusis, tetanus, polio, measles, mumps, rubella, typhoid and hepatitis-B.
- Breast feeding is important for the mother and the child.
- Mother childhood ailments like seasing, sore eyes, earache, chickenpox, influenza, diarrhoea, dysentery can be easily managed.

8

Aspects of Development

Introduction

Little children are remarkably adult miniatures. Child is very soft delicate, charming lovable and helpless, but children are helpless because he/she still needs to given and develop in order to be independent individuals. When will the child be independent? A child will be independent when he/she can perform skills communicate/speak and understand the difference between right and wrong.

Children grow and develop slowly and gradually. If you observed a child closely, you will be able to notice the various stages of growth and development. After reading this chapter you will be able to:

- Enlist the various aspects of growth and development.
- Understand that physical development brings about changes in height, weight, body proportions and teaching.
- Understand that child's ability to control toilet functions comes with physical and muscular control.
- Describe the motor development of children from birth to three years to age.

- Explain the social and emotional development of children upto three years of age.
- Define socialization.
- Explain development of language and cognition of different stages up to 3 years.

What is Child Development?

Child development refers to how a child becomes able to do more complex things as they get older. Development is different than growth. Growth only refers to the child getting bigger in size. When we talk about normal development, we are talking about developing skills like:

- **Gross Motor:** Using large groups of muscles to sit, stand, walk, run, etc., keeping balance, and changing positions.
- **Fine Motor:** Using hands to be able to eat, draw, dress, play, write, and do many other things.
- **Language:** Speaking, using body language and gestures, communicating, and understanding what others say.
- **Cognitive:** Thinking skills: including learning, understanding, problem-solving, reasoning, and remembering.
- **Social:** Interacting with others, having relationships with family, friends, and teachers, cooperating, and responding to the feelings of others.

What are Developmental Milestones?

Developmental milestones are a set of functional skills or age-specific tasks that most children can do at a certain age range. Your pediatrician uses milestones to help check how your child is developing. Although each milestone has an age level, the actual age when a normally developing child reaches that milestone can very quite a bit. Every child is unique!

Assessing Child's Development

Assessing your child's development is a team effort. Your family plays an important role. At your child's well-child visit, your pediatrician will spend time watching them and talking with you to find out about what your child is doing since your last visit. Tell your child's doctor about any worries or concerns you may have. Your pediatrician may also use developmental screening in the office. Screening involves a series of questions and observations that gets at your child's ability to perform certain age-appropriate tasks. Using developmental milestones as a guide can help pediatricians identify children who may be at risk for developmental delay.

Various Aspects of Growth and Development

Growth and development are generally used together to refer to the various aspects of an children overall performance. The various aspects are as follows:

(a) Physical development.

(b) Emotional development.

(c) Muscular development.

(d) Cognitive development.

(e) Social development.

(f) Language development.

(g) Moral development.

(a) **Physical Development**: It refers to changes in height and weight and the associated changes in shape and size of the child.

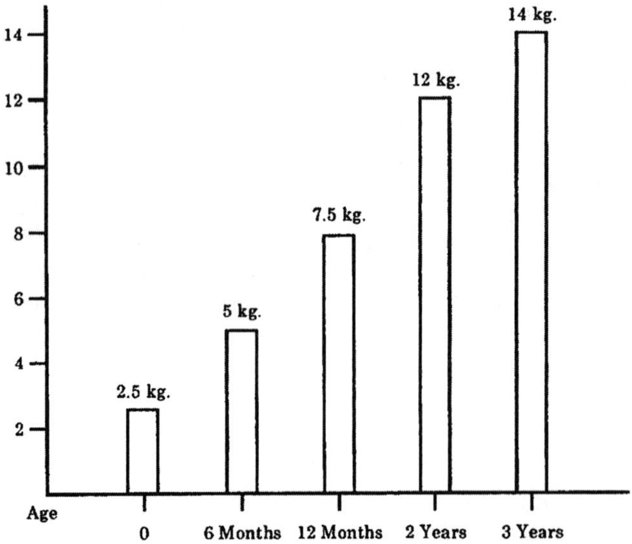

There are changes in the body proportions as well. The approximate weight of an Indian child at birth 2.5 kg. The initial doubles by the time the child in 6 months of age. The birth weight treables by the time the child is one year old. At two and three years, the child weights approximately 12 kg and 14 kg respectly.

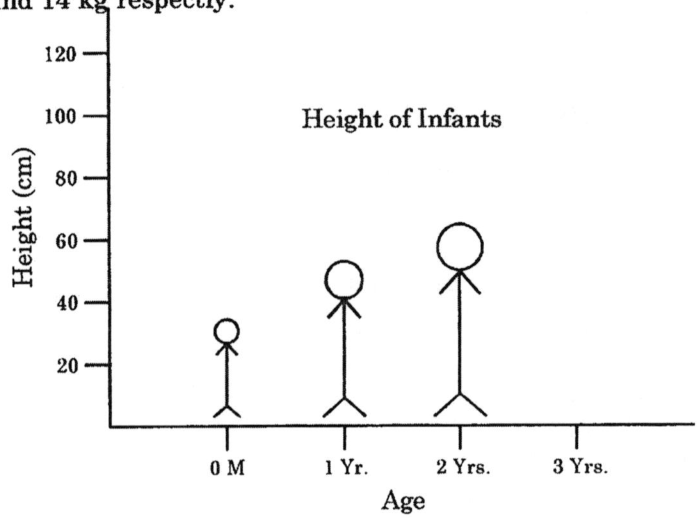

The average height of an Indian baby at birth is 50 cms. Do you know-how much a child grows in the first year of life? A one year old baby is 20-25 cms more than his/her height at birth two years old child measures 82-85 cms in height. Hereafter the child grow by approximately 8-10 cms per year.

In the foetal state the hands and legs are small and the trunk is like a bag. The head is ¼ the body size. The legs and hands grow at a faster rate during infancy. Consequently the body proportion show considerable improvement as an be seen in the diagram.

Development of teeth is an important aspect of physical growth.

The human beings get two sets of teeth in life (a) The primary set/ baby/baby teeth/ milkteeth. (b) The permanent teeth, i.e.,120 teeth.

Primary Set of Teeth

Eruption of Teeth	*Age*
Two middle lower incisors	6-8 months
Four upper incisors	8-12 months
Lateral incisors	12-14 months
Four first molars	12-15 months
Four canivers	18-20 months
Four second molars	20-24 months

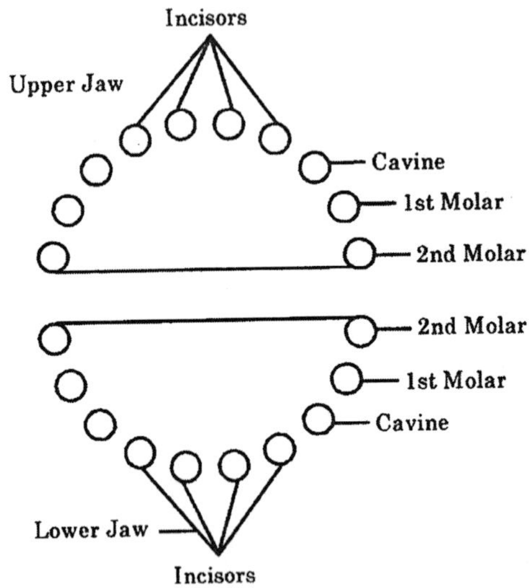

(b) **Emotional Development**: Joy, anger, fear and happiness are some of the emotions that can be noticed even among small children. The emotions are simple reactions that suggests pleasure and displeasure. Sucking at mother's breast, rocking and holding the baby make the child happy. Sudden loud noise and wet diapers cause fear and make the child cry. The emotional expressions change with age.

(c) **Muscular Development**: The bones become strong with calcium deposits. The muscles attached to bones facilitate movement. Do you remember the different kinds of muscles? The muscles become bigger and storonger with age. Muscles enables children to perform tougher jobs with each passing year. The full potential is reached by adolescence.

Physical and muscular developments are together referred to as motor development. Toilet control develops with physical and muscular development, mothers should ensure to keep the baby clean and dry. Toilet training can be initiated as early as six months of age. The child can be made to sit an the specially designed toilet seat at regular intervals.

Children are in total control of bowel movement and urination by the time 2 to 2½ years old. They are now ready to go to play schools.

(d) **Cognitive Development**: Cognitive development refers to the process of learning and understanding. It is connected with the function of the brain. If you ask a small child to give his/her rattle to you, in all probability you will have no reaction because the child has not understood you. The cognition develop of with age. Cognition leads to development of language amongst infants.

(e) **Social Development**: Infants do not show interest in their environment. They are quite content when fed and kept clean and dry. As the child grow he/she starts noticing and recognising the mother and all those around him/her in the home. Ability to notice others marks the onset of social development.

(f) **Language Development**: Little infants can only produce gurgling and cooing sounds. As they give the babies start making short and simple word sounds like Ma-ma, Ta-ta, Cha-cha, Ba-ba and Pa-pa etc. This starts the language development which improves with age and repetitive use.

(g) **Moral Development**: Small children do not have the ability to discriminate between good and bad or right and wrong. Parents, siblings and family members are the role models for the small child. As the cognitive development improves the child learns to discriminate between good and bad. This starts the moral development of the child at home. It is thus important that the elders around the child show good behaviour.

The various aspects of growth and development occurs at the same time resulting in the overall development of the child.

Characteristics of Motor Development

Little children slowly and gradually lead to control and coordinate the difference body parts.

"Motor development refers to the infant ability to use muscles and bones to perform different skills."

The average motor development of young children at different ages is generally referred to as the "milestones." The milestones are the same for all infants. However, a certain degree of variation may be noticed among different children, Little delay in the achievement milestones is no cause to worry. The motor development changes can be noticed every 3-4 weeks. These changes as being discussed belong:

Age 0 to 3 Years

1st month children at birth are helpless beings. The child starts holding head from the age of one month onwards. The neck of infants is hardly visible because the skin folds cover it.

Second Month: 2 months old baby can raise his/her chest and head while lying on the abdomen.

Third Month: 3 months child tries to reach out to the object hold near him/her. However, he/she misses to hold the object because of inadequate focusing of vision. Neck starts being visible from 3 months. Child can caught smiling.

4th—5th Months: Children start sitting and complete head control, grass small objects hold blocks, use specific fingers, thumb to hold play material.

6th Month: Independently sit in a chair grasp objects. They can hold bottle on cup to their mouth for drinking water and milk.

7th Month: Child's ability to sit independently is remarkable. Infant capable of shifting from lying position to sitting and back again to lying.

8th—9th Months: Children start using legs to move around in their "walker". The child tirles to stand by holding the objects in his/her environment, i.e. table, chair etc. Child starts crawling on abdomen.

10—12 Months: The child is able to creep and crawl better on his/her hands and kees children learn to stand with confidence. The child feels happy to stand and hold hands of parents and siblings. He/she tries to take a few steps with their help. The parents also feel thrilled when the initial walking steps are taken by their loved one.

Age 1 Yr.—2 Yrs: Child has total control to sit and walk independently. The child now starts exploring environment by trying to move up the steps. Climb the steps at this age is not without hazards. Some toddlers can ride tricylers by the age of two years.

Age 2 Yrs.—3 Yrs: Motor development shows considerable improvement an account of physical and muscular maturity, children can run and play, jump, playing football, more grasping power, balance on tip and toes, dressing himself, better coordination of hands. All motor skills improve with practice, Hence children should be encouraged to play and understand the environment.

Essential in Learning Motor Skills

(a) **Readiness to Learn:** The learning of any skill is superior and easy when the child, is ready for it. For example, when is the child ready for walking? The answer is when the child's leg muscles are developed enough to support his/her weight.

(b) **Opportunity to Learn:** Many parents are afraid that their child will get hurt thus depriving the child of the opportunity to learn.

(c) **Opportunity to Practice:** The children should be given sufficient time to master the skill. For example, the child staggers and sway when he/she starts walking. Practising this makes them walk without staggering.

(d) **Good Models:** Children learn skills by initiating. Have you even seen that a walking child starts according on seeing a small baby doing so? Children must be provided with good role models to imitate.

(e) **Guidance:** Children guidance to initiate models. It helps them to correct errors before they are so well learned that it is difficult to change.

(f) **Motivation:** Motivation is essential for learning motor skills. Children derive satisfaction and independence by learning the various motor skills. Encourage them to master skills each motor skill must be learnt individual.

(g) **Skills should be Learnt One at a Time:** Learning different skills involving the same muscle are often confusing and yield poor results. Hence the self feeding and colouring skills should be learnt one at a time.

Factors Affecting Skills

- Retarded growth.
- Poor health and low energy.
- Low mental ability and same handicap.
- Lack of opportunity.
- Insufficient and inadequate guidance.
- Low motivation.
- Tear of being different.

Characteristics of Social Development

Social development refers to the ability of a child to behave in a manner acceptable to the society in which he/she lives. Social development leads to socialisation. Socialization is a process where by the child learns to eat, speaks and play. It also means behaving well in a group.

Age 0—3 Months: They are happy as long as they are fed and clean. They starts recognising sounds. They start responding by smiling.

Age 4—6 Months: The infants become more social now. They notice the individuals around then. They respond by gurgling, cooing and babbling.

Age 7—9 Months: The bonds between the infant and the mother or mother figure are stronger during this period. They can differentiate between love and scolding.

Age 10—18 Months: These older infants feel secure with family members and avoid strangers. They become possessive of things belonging to the mother/parents. They are antisocial and will not part with their toys. These children indulge in individual play and have very little interaction with other children.

Age 1½ to 3 Years: The feelings to possesion are strong to the extent that the child wants the mother's and divided attention. Socially the parents will have problems if there are siblings in the family, children learn to socialise by observing people in their environment, slowly and gradually they acquire accepted social relationships. Such children will be afraid to do anything an their own and hence become socially dependent. Parents should also guide and encourage children to learn good social behaviour.

Some Important Skills of Early Childhoods

(a) Self Help Skills

Bathing, dressing, feeding, self grooming, self-toileting.

(b) Social Skills

Looking after toys, house help (to help mother).

(c) Play Skills

Hands skills, leg skill.

(d) Work Skills

Drawing lines, writing.

Characteristics of Emotional Development

Emotions are feeling everyone is born with. "Emotional development means the ability to control emotions and express them in ways acceptable to the society."

Age 0—3 Months: Children feel distressed when hungry and wet. They feel delighted when talked to in soft tones. They express their feeling by crying and smiling.

Age 4—6 Months: Children showing anger when they are wet, hungry and do not find mother around them.

Age 7—9 Months: The development of bonds between mother, child show affection, emotion is expressed by hugging, cudding. They do not being separated from them.

Age 10—18 Months: Children are worry of strangers, they get scared, they fear the absence of mother. Extreme fear and anger leads to crying amongs children.

Age 1½—3 Years: The child becomes jealous of the siblings when the mother attends to their needs. This emotions may cause bed-wetting and thumb sucking among children. Children often break things and become destructive to attract attention. Emotional behaviour varies amongst children. Emotions are shortlived. The various agents helping in the socialization process of the child are parents, siblings and peers around the house. The teacher, other classmates, help the child to develop socially in case the child attends the play schools and Balwadi.

Characteristics of Cognitive Development

"Cognitive development refers to the ability of the child to think and find solution to problems." It involves changes occurring in the mental ability of a child such as thinking, reasoning and finding away to solve the problem.

Age 0—3 Months: The cognitive development of the new born is extremely limited. The child satisfy hunger by sucking instinctively. The child circles and the mother feeds the baby. Slowly the child start correlating crying with being fed. The child can also be seen moving lips when hungry.

Age 4—6 Months: Cognition takes time to develop whatever is held by the child is take to the mouth and sucking starts. In due course the child learns that the "rattle" or the "ball" that he/she holds cannot give milk to satisfy the hunger.

Age 7—12 Months: Children development curiosity in this stage. It is very apparent that cognition is modifying child's behaviour.

Age 1 Yr—3 Yrs: The child comes crying to the mother that he/she has been hit by the table. If the tricycle is damaged he/she may force the mother to tie a bandage around its handle, that means child's cognition is developing. He/

she can now identify hurt with pain and bandage with relief. Slowly and gradually the children are able to mentally conserve their experiences and use them to solve problems. Cognition develops further with the increasing age of sensory organs.

Characteristics of Language Development

"Language development means the ability to communicate through the use of meaningful words and sentences."

Age 0—3 Months: The only sound that the child can produce is of "crying". By crying they communicate to their mother that they are heavy on well. By the time they are 3 months old they respond by cooing and learn to produce the "caoo" sounds. The children make gurgling sounds when they are well-fed and happy.

Age 4—6 Months: The children of this age group start producing flat "a-a" sounds. Gradually the child starts producing various sounds like pa, ma, ta ba, na and so on.

Age 7—9 Months: The child now produces double flat sounds like baba, mama, nana and papa etc. Such sounds produced by the baby are often referred to as "babbling." The child learns to say tall, hall, baja, dalla etc. A baby learns to associate meaning with an object and then a word becomes a symbol on lable for the object.

Age 10—12 Months: The children now start speaking in simple sentences. A child who say's "babi-ball" or "babi doll" actually means "baby's" ball and "baby's doll." The language develops with repeated usage. The child reproduces sounds by initiating.

Age 1—2 Years: The children now are promoted to three-four word sentences. They can now say, "I want doll" and "U want a big doll" and "I want red doll." An 18-20 months old child can speak about 50 words.

Age 2—3 Years: The children have a habit of using the namely learnt words repeatedly. They copy sounds and behave like parrots. They just don't tire of receiving nursery rhymes learnt at home are play schools. They are even ready to show off their language skills, children learn to speak more than one language quite easily. The child speak one language at home and the other to communicate with playmates outside the house. They can have a vocabulary of above 1000 words

General Development at the Age of 1st Year

Your child is going through many physical and mental changes. Although no two children grow at the same rate, experts agree there are "normal" signs of development. This will show you important milestones in your child's development during the first year of life. It is a simple tool you can use to become aware of and appreciate the dramatic changes that are occurring in your child.

Watch for these signs in your child over a one month period (Even children have "bad days"). Remember, each child is different and may learn and grow at a different rate. However, if your child cannot do many of the skills listed for his or her age group, you should consult your pediatrician. If your child was born sooner than expected, be sure to deduct the number of months early from his or her age. A 5 month-old born 2 months early would be expected to show the same skills as a 3 month-old who was born on his or her due date. You are the most important observer of your child's development. If your child has special needs, early help can make a difference.

By 3 Months of Age Activity of Child

Motor Skills

- Lift head when held at your shoulder
- Lift head and chest when lying on his stomach

- Turn head from side to side when lying on his stomach
- Follow a moving object or person with his eyes
- Often hold hands open or loosely fisted
- Grasp rattle when given to her
- Wiggle and kick with arms and legs

Sensory and Thinking Skills

- Turn head toward bright colours and lights
- Turn toward the sound of a human voice
- Recognize bottle or breast
- Respond to your shaking a rattle or bell

Language and Social Skills

- Make cooing, gurgling sounds
- Smile when smiled at
- Communicate hunger, fear, discomfort (through crying or facial expression)
- Usually quiet down at the sound of a soothing voice or when held
- Anticipate being lifted
- React to "peek-a-boo" games

By 6 Months of Age Activity of Child

Motor Skills

- Hold head steady when sitting with your help
- Reach for and grasp objects

- Play with his toes
- Help hold the bottle during feeding
- Explore by mouthing and banging objects
- Move toys from one hand to another
- Shake a rattle
- Pull up to a sitting position on her own if you grasp her hands
- Sit with only a little support
- Sit in a high chair
- Roll over
- Bounce when held in a standing position

Sensory and Thinking Skills

- Open his mouth for the spoon
- Imitate familiar actions you perform

Language and Social Skills

- Babble, making almost sing-song sounds
- Know familiar faces
- Laugh and squeal with delight
- Scream if annoyed
- Smile at herself in a mirror

By 12 Months of Age Activity of Child

Motor Skills

- Drink from a cup with help

- Feed herself finger food like raisins or bread crumbs
- Grasp small objects by using her thumb and index or forefinger
- Use his first finger to poke or point
- Put small blocks in and take them out of a container
- Knock two blocks together
- Sit well without support
- Crawl on hands and knees
- Pull himself to stand or take steps holding onto furniture
- Stand alone momentarily
- Walk with one hand held
- Cooperate with dressing by offering a foot or an arm

Sensory and Thinking Skills

- Copy sounds and actions you make
- Respond to music with body motion
- Try to accomplish simple goals (seeing and then crawling to a toy)
- Look for an object she watched fall out of sight (such as a spoon that falls under the table)

Language and Social Skills

- Babble, but it sometimes "sounds like" talking
- Say his first word
- Recognize family members' names

- Try to "talk" with you
- Respond to another's distress by showing distress or crying
- Show affection to familiar adults
- Show mild to severe anxiety at separation from parent
- Show apprehension about strangers
- Raise her arms when she wants to be picked up
- Understand simple commands

General Development at the Age of 2 Years

Your child is going through many physical and mental changes. Although no two children grow at the same rate, experts agree there are "normal" signs of development.

It is a simple tool you can use to become aware of and appreciate the dramatic changes that are occurring in your child. Watch for these signs in your child over a one month period (Even children have "bad days"). Remember, each child is different and may learn and grow at a different rate. However, if your child cannot do many of the skills listed for his or her age group, you should consult your pediatrician. If your child was born sooner than expected, be sure to deduct the number of months early from his or her age. A 5-month-old born 2 months early would be expected to show the same skills as a 3-month-old who was born on his or her due date. You are the most important observer of your child's development. If your child has special needs, early help can make a difference.

By 18 Months of Age Activity of Child

Motor Skills

- Like to pull, push, and dump things

- Pull off hat, socks, and mittens
- Turn pages in a book
- Stack 2 blocks
- Carry a stuffed animal or doll
- Scribble with crayons
- Walk without help
- Run stiffly, with eyes on the ground

Sensory and Thinking Skills

- Identify an object in a picture book
- Laugh at silly actions (as in wearing a bowl as a hat)
- Look for objects that are out of sight
- Put a round lid on a round pot
- Follow simple 1-step directions
- Solve problems by trial and error

Language and Social Skills

- Say 8-10 words you can understand
- Look at a person who is talking to him
- Ask specifically for her mother or father
- Use "hi," "bye," and "please," with reminders
- Protest when frustrated
- Ask for something by pointing or by using one word
- Direct another's attention to an object or action

- Become anxious when separated from parent(s)
- Seek attention
- Bring toys to share with parentact out a familiar activity in play (as in pretending to take a bath)
- Play alone on the floor with toys
- Compete with other children for toys
- Recognize herself in the mirror or in pictures
- Seem selfish at times

By 2 Years of Age Activity of Child

Motor Skills

- Drink from a straw
- Feed himself with a spoon
- Help in washing hands
- Put arms in sleeves with help build a tower of 3-4 blocks
- Toss or roll a large ball
- Open cabinets, drawers, boxes
- Operate a mechanical toy
- Bend over to pick up a toy and not fall
- Walk up steps with help
- Take steps backward

Sensory and Thinking Skills

- Like to take things apart

- Explore surroundings
- Point to 5-6 parts of a doll when asked

Language and Social Skills

- Have a vocabulary of several hundred words
- Use 2-3 word sentences
- Say names of toys
- Ask for information about an object (asks, "Shoe?" while pointing to shoe box)
- Hum or try to sing
- Listen to short rhymes
- Like to imitate parents
- Sometimes get angry and have temper tantrums
- Act shy around strangers
- Comfort a distressed friend or parent
- Take turns in play with other children
- Treat a doll or stuffed animal as though it were alive
- Apply pretend action to others (as in pretending to feed a doll)
- Show awareness of parental approval or disapproval for her actions
- Refer to self by name and use "me" and "mine"
- Verbalize his desires and feelings ("I want cookie")

- Laugh at silly labelling of objects and events (as in calling a nose an ear)
- Enjoy looking at one book over and over
- Point to eyes, ears, or nose when you ask

What are Speech and Language

Speech and language are tools that humans use to communicate or share thoughts, ideas, and emotions. Language is the set of rules, shared by the individuals who are communicating, that allows them to exchange those thoughts, ideas, or emotions. Speech is talking, one way that a language can be expressed. Language may also be expressed through writing, signing, or even gestures in the case of people who have neurological disorders and may depend upon eye blinks or mouth movements to communicate.

While there are many languages in the world, each includes its own set of rules for phonology (phonemes or speech sounds or, in the case of signed language, handshapes), morphology (word formation), syntax (sentence formation), semantics (word and sentence meaning), prosody (intonation and rhythm of speech), and pragmatics (effective use of language).

Speech and Language Develop: Normally

The most intensive period of speech and language development for humans is during the first three years of life, a period when the brain is developing and maturing. These skills appear to develop best in a world that is rich with sounds, sights, and consistent exposure to the speech and language of others.

There is increasing evidence suggesting that there are "critical periods" for speech and language development in infants and young children. This means that the developing brain is best able to absorb a language, any language, during this period. The ability to learn a language will be more difficult, and perhaps less efficient or effective, if these critical periods are allowed to pass without early exposure to a language. The beginning signs of communication occur during the first few days of life when an infant learns that a cry will bring food, comfort, and companionship. The newborn also begins to recognize important sounds in his or her environment. The sound of a parent or voice can be one important sound. As they grow, infants begin to sort out the speech sounds (phonemes) or building blocks that compose the words of their language. Research has shown that by six months of age, most children recognize the basic sounds of their native language.

As the speech mechanism (jaw, lips, and tongue) and voice mature, an infant is able to make controlled sound. This begins in the first few months of life with "cooing," a quiet, pleasant, repetitive vocalization. By six months of age, an infant usually babbles or produces repetitive syllables such as "ba, ba, ba" or "da, da, da." Babbling soon turns into a type of nonsense speech (jargon) that often has the tone and cadence of human speech but does not contain real words. By the end of their first year, most children have mastered the ability to say a few simple words. Children are most likely unaware of the meaning of their first words, but soon learn the power of those words as others respond to them.

By eighteen months of age, most children can say eight to ten words. By age two, most are putting words together in crude sentences such as "more milk." During this period, children rapidly learn that words symbolize or represent objects, actions, and thoughts. At this age they also engage in representational or pretend play. At ages three, four, and five, a child's vocabulary rapidly increases, and he or she begins to master the rules of language.

Developmental Milestones of Speech and Language

Children vary in their development of speech and language. There is, however, a natural progression or "timetable" for mastery of these skills for each language. The milestones are identifiable skills that can serve as a guide to normal development. Typically, simple skills need to be reached before the more complex skills can be learned. There is a general age and time when most children pass through these periods. These milestones help doctors and other health professionals determine when a child may need extra help to learn to speak or to use language

Child's Delayed Speech or Language

You should talk to your family doctor if you have any concerns about your child's speech or language development. The above checklist should help you talk about your concerns. Your doctor may decide to refer you to a speech-language pathologist, a health professional trained to evaluate and treat people who have speech, language, voice or swallowing disorders (including hearing impairment) that affect their ability to communicate. The speech-language pathologist will talk to you about your child's communication and general development. He or she will also evaluate your child with special speech and language tests. A hearing test is often included in the evaluation because a hearing problem can affect speech and language development.

Depending upon the test results, the speech-language pathologist may suggest activities for home to stimulate speech and language development. These activities may include reading to your child regularly; speaking in short sentences using simple words so that your child can successfully imitate you; or repeating what your child says, using correct grammar or pronunciation. For example, if your child says, "Ball baybo" you can respond with, "Yes, the ball is under the table." This allows you to demonstrate more accurate speech and language without actually "correcting" your child which can eventually make speaking unpleasant for him or her.

The speech-language pathologist may also recommend group or individual therapy or suggest further evaluation by other health professionals such as an audiologist, a health care professional who is trained to identify and measure hearing loss, or a developmental psychologist.

9

Special Needs of Disadvantaged Children

Introduction

The children grow and develop physically, socially and emotionally "Each Individual is like all other people like some other people and like no other person."

All children are "Unique" yet similar to one another in most aspects of growth. However some children are very different from their age mates that they "standout". The "Standout" creates problems during the growing periods. Such children have to deal with the normal/usual problems of growth along with all those difficulties that may arise because to being different.

The child's ability to cope with these problems is limited. The child is unable to deal with the social and emotional problems. This has marked effect on the child's personal and social development. Such a child needs special attention during the formative years so as to be able to give to the full potential.

Normal Child and Disabled/Disadvantage Child

A normal healthy child is able to give out and do things to equip for future life. A child who is not able to withstand the challenge of day to day life is generally referred to as handicapped/disabled or disadvantaged child.

According to psychologists a normal child can be defined "as one who is physically socially, mentally, intellectually and morally adjusted and is in harmony with oneself and his/her surrounding environment. Such a child is able to conform to the norms of the particular society.

According to Baker, a well known psychologist defines the disabled child as "one who deviates from what is supposed to be an average in physical, mental, emotional and social characters to such an extent that the child requires special educational services to help develop to the maximum "capacity".

Categories of Disabled/Disadvantaged Children

The disabled children can be broadly grouped into three catogories. These are:

(a) Physically handicapped children.

(b) Mentally disadvantaged children.

(c) Socially Mal-adjusted children.

Causes of Disability Among Children

The various causes of physical disability area as follows:

(a) Heredity.

(b) Unfavourable Prenatal environment.

(c) Injury during child birth.

(d) Accident during early childhood causing or orthopaedic problems.

(e) Surgery requiring the amputation of the diseased part.

(f) Mental and emotional problems in early childhood result in stammering, stuttering and speech defects.

(g) Ear infections and injuries resulting in hearing defects.

(h) Psychological emotional problems and feelings of neglect result in behavioural problems. Such children are not able to keep up with the desired social norms and hence are at disadvantage.

(i) Imaginary defects called "phantom handicaps" occur when small children imagine they are handicapped and demand to be excused from doing things they do not want to do.

Types of Disabled Handicaps

Handicaps result in physical, neurological and social maladjustment and defects.

(a) Physical Defects

(i) Defect in eyes (Blind and partially).

(ii) Defect in ears (Deaf and hard of hearing).

(iii) Missing limb/weak limb.

(iv) Physical abnormalities such as webbed fingers, hunch, sixth finger mal-formed ear, harelip, cleft plate, and birth marks.

(v) Defective speech—it results in stammering that affects child's personality.

(vi) Chronical defects—Congenital heart disease, rheumatism and nuclear atrophy.

(b) Neurological Defects

These are caused by disorders of the central nervous system, e.g., cerebral palsy, epilepsy, and schizophrenia;

cerebral palsy results in paralysis/motion disorder of limbs due to brain malfunction. Sudden uncontrollable attacks (seizures) resulting in loss of consciousness and muscle control are common among epileptic patients.

These defects can be corrected/improved to a great extent when defected and treated in time medical, surgical and scientific advancement is providing tremendous inprovements to cope with the different handicaps.

(c) Social Maladjustment Defect

Socially maladjusted children do not conform to the acceptable social norms of the society. The children can be indulging in antisocial activities leading to juvenile delinquency and other related problems. Socially disadvantaged child is a deprived child improved of love, proper guidance and general social security.

Reactions of adults around the handicapped children have a different influence on their personal and social adjustments.

What is Disadvantaged?

A child is considered disadvantaged:

(a) Child cannot make the maximum use of one on several of the senses, e.g., blind child, deaf and mute child.

(b) Child is not able to adjust well in the society one lives in. Such a child will exhibit behavioural problems.

(c) Child who is able to make sharper use of senses, e.g., exceptional/bright child can also be disadvantaged.

Blindness

Vision is a critical tool that children use in obtaining information about the world in which they live. Impairment of vision can lead to partial or total blindness. The children without vision will need special material and attention to developfully. A blind child is not able to compete with the normal one. As a result these children may remain physically and economically dependent to a certain extent.

Causes of Blindness

Visual impairment can be caused by the following factors:

(a) Congenital Blindness

It refers to a child being born blind. Genetic impairment results in the malformation of vital organ like eyes during the foetal development. Such children learn about their environment through the senses of tough and hearing.

(b) Acquired Blindness

Child is not born blind. The child may lose eyesight on account of some accident. Children playing with bow and arrow often suffer serious eye injuries resulting eye defect is called acquired advantitious blindness.

(c) Nutritional Blindness

It is a result of prolonged absence of vitamin A rich foods in the diet. Deficiency of vitamin A causes dryness of eyes, and impaired vision in dimlight (night blindness). Poor state of epithelial tissues coupled with resulting eye infections causes serious damage to the eyes.

(d) Delayed Remedial Treatment

Poverty, ıgnorance and superstitious are responsible for delayed medical treatment. Lack of proper medical facilities also add to eye related problems. India's blind population forms a major chunk of world's total.

Measurement of Vision

Snullen's test is used to measure the sight. Snullen's chart bearing letters/digits of different size are kept at a distance of 6 meters from the individual whose sight to be tested.

2
0 5
3 6 4
7 9 5 2
6 0 3 2 2
1 0 3 4 5

Characteristics of a Partially Blind Child

(i) A partially child is clumsy, awkward and cautious in his/her movements.

(ii) The eyes may be red, watery, swollen, iching and sensitive to light.

(iii) Child may complain of headache, ransea and blurring of vision.

(iv) Child may have squint and appear "cross-eyed".

(v) Poor vision makes the child irritable, self centered and pre-occupied.

(vi) Child has fewer opportunities to learn to get along with different social groups. This results in social adjustment problems.

(vii) The children become rebellious and aggressive for they have to rely on others to do things for them, This often leads to frustration and inferiority complex among them.

Special Needs of a Blind Child

It is important or render all possible help and attention to the blind child to enable him/her to be independent, self reliant and economically viable. Physical, social and emotional needs have to be attended with special attention to yield satisfying results.

Physical Needs: Parents of a young blind child have to give special attention to feed and cloth their little one. Children need to be trained to do their daily routine jobs like toilet, bath, dressing and feeding etc. Special effforts needed to help them move around the house without looking things and highly themselves. Orientation and mobility training for such children is a must from the early age. These children must be made familiar and comfortable with their bodies and the surroundings may live in the parents may need to take these children often to the doctors to protect them from disease arising out of general constitutional weakness.

Emotional and Social Needs

Parents and siblings need to develop special contact by hugging, petting and reassuring the handicapped child when scared and emotionally upset. Constant reassurance with love and tender care will help the disadvantaged child in exercising better control on emotions and feel emotionally secure.

Every child needs to be loved to feel secure. This enables one to interact in a correct way and with confidence. A blind child's social world is his/her parents. Parent's attitude and acceptance of the disability of their child goes a long way in providing the child with confidence to deal with the routine problems. It must be accepted that total development of the child is slower when compared to a normal child. The need to love and Beloved is slowly among handicapped children. The strong bonds of love help the child intake bigger leaps in the process of development. Consequently the child will be well-adjusted in his/her social environment. Social and emotional adjustments are essential for disadvantaged children.

Independence Need: The parents should help the child to explore his/her surroundings and do routine jobs independently. To start with combing hair, buttoning up of shirt and trying of shoe laces, etc. may be time consuming and clumpy. Appreciation will encourage the child to take on new jobs with confidence. The child's need to feel capable can be enhanced by providing vocational guidance for the jobs he/she can perform. This will ensure self reliance. Have you ever noticed the "while" stick used by the blind to move around? The stick may be fitted with bell.

Educational Needs: It is posible to educate children with poor sight, total partial blindness books with big print and desk with proper light are of considerable help to the child with defective vision. Green/grey board instead of a blackboard, unglazed paper and use of soft black pensils improve the visibility for such a child. Handicapped children learn better with special equipment under the guidance of special educators.

Children with severe defects will need to be educated with special tools like "BRAILLE", (Braille system dots punched, use for reading/writing letters/digits for blind). Blind children need to develop listening skills to better their learning.

Special attention is being given to the blind children in the form of education and training. More employment opportunities provided to the blind adults are an assurance of their legal and human rights.

Deafness

New born infants are able to respond to the sound by starting and blinking of eyes. As they grow they recognise their parents' voices and enjoy their own cooing and gurgling sounds, listening leads to language development later the children learn to attach meaning to sound.

Children born with hearing impairment are unable to learn for they have not heard the sound to which they can attach meaning. This results in communication barrier.

Deaf and Hard of Hearing

A deaf child is one who has last the sense of hearing before learning the language. This means that the child is born without the ability to hear. Such children are often mute and silent.

Hard of hearing on the other hand is a defect that is acquired later in life. The child experiences varying degrees of hearing loss.

Causes of Deafness and Hearing Loss

Hearing impairment and loss are due to the following factors:

(a) Conductive deafness is better understood when you are acquinted with the structure of the ear. The sound is conducted through the air into the outer ear. On reaching the tympanic membrane the sound waves change the fluid level in semicircular overall. The passage of air in the outer ear is called the "conductive pathway."

The conductive pathway can get affected due to:

(i) Build up of wax in the ear.

(ii) A foreign body in the pathway, and

(iii) Any swelling of the outer ear.

These conditions can cause temporary deafness that can be medically treated. Conductive deafness causes blockage of the drained tube. The blocking fluid becomes thick like "glue" can be drained out with surgical operation.

(b) Sensory Neural Deafness is due to the damage of the ear drum, cochlea, auditory move and associated brain cells. Such a damage can be (i) congenital or (ii) acquired.

(i) **Congenital deafness** can be due to genetic disorders and premature birth. A pregnant mother having German measles during the first trimester of pragnacy may give birth to deaf child. An attack of severe jaundice in which the mother's blood is incompatible with that of the foetus also results in congenital deafness

(ii) **Acquired deafness** is due to viral infection such as mumps, measles, influenza, and meningitis in early childhood. These viral infections are responsible for sensory neural deafness.

(c) **Mixed hearing loss** is a result of hearing impairement arising due to a combinations of conductive and sensory neural defects.

Measurement of Hearing Loss

The hearing loss can be measured in terms of child's ability to respond to the various sounds.

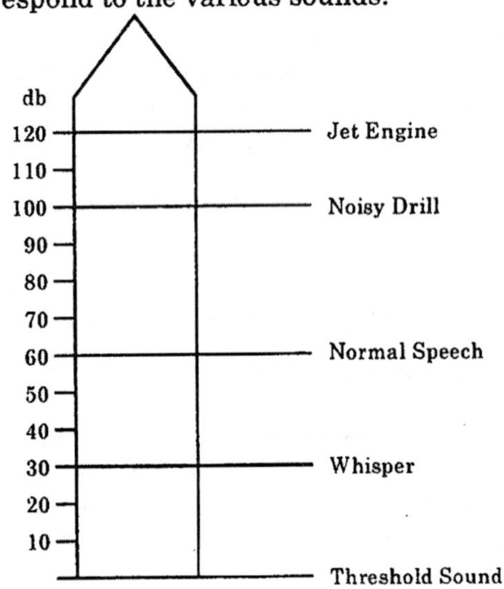

(Levels of Intensity of Sound)

The terms "Intensity" refers to soft, medium, loud and harsh sounds etc. While "Frequency" refers to the number of vibrations produced per second by a particular sound. The increase in frequency is accompanied by a rise in the pitch.

The sound is measured in terms of decibel (dB). A device called the "Audiometer" is used to measure the ability to hear. Child's responses to different sounds are recorded on the audiometer and compared with average normal value.

- Slightly impaired hearing is when the child does not respond to sound than 40 dB
- Moderately impaired hearing is when the child does not respond to sound upto 70 dB
- Severe hearing impairment is the inability of the child to respond sounds less than 95 dB

Characteristics of a Deaf Child

- The child may be dumb besides being deaf.
- The speech defects are common among child with hearing impairment.
- They have difficulty in learning language/ vocabulary. It is an enormous challenge to learn to communicate in a language one cannot hear.
- Consequently these children are low in intelligence because they are incapable of using available opportunities.
- Such children have suspicious minds because of lack of coordination between vision and hearing. This also results in their inability to make friends.
- A deaf child is often indifferent and stubborn.
- Sensitivity to hearing impairment among children leads to frustrations and inferiority complex.

The resultant poor. Communication causes tremendous socializing problems.

Special Needs of a Deaf Child

Hearing defects causes a lot of problems ranging from language and vocabulary to comprehension and communication.

(1) **Physical needs** can be effectively taken care of by providing physical comfort to enable these children to improve their listening skills. Parents can help the child to locate sounds, i.e., running of water to the tap or ringing of bell to the door. Intelligent parents can use playway techniques to help child recognise the sound, e.g., hiding a musical toy and encouraging the child to look for it.

The child is helped to discriminate the sound, e.g., difference between father's and mother's voice, singing and carrying etc.

The next step is the recognition of speech sounds. It is directly influenced by child's ability to use vision and other senses.

(2) **Emotional and Social Needs:** Suspicion is almost the second nature both deaf children. Consequently they get emotionally up tight. Their social behaviour also needs to be improved and refined.

(3) **Love Needs:** Need to love and be loved is an important for these children as it is for the blind. Love and affection provide emotional security besides the much needed encouragement for better learning.

(4) **Educational Needs:** It involves child's ability to understand the language. They learn to communicate through visual and manual means.

(5) **Oral Method on Lip Reading:** It is a special way of educating deaf children to identify sounds by watching the lip movements. It is a slow method involving a lot of patience for the learner as well as the educator.

(6) **Manual Method or Sign Language:** It helps the child to communicate with gestures, cues and finger spellings. You have watch on the news bulletin.

(7) **Need to be Independent:** It is of upmost importance to the deaf child. It reduces his/her dependency on parents, and siblings. The ability to be independent makes them important components of the society they live in. Invention of hearing aids have provided the much need relief to the deaf.

Causes of Affected and Missing Limb

A child with affected limb is not able to perform fully the activities involving the use of bones, muscles and joints. Similar handicap is experienced by children with the missing limb. Such children are known to be or orthopaedically crippled.

The famous psychologist "Cruickshank" defines a child with effected and missing limb "as one who has a defect which causes a deformity or an interference with the normal functioning of bone, muscle or joint." Such orthopaedic (bony) conditions may be congenital or acquired.

(a) **Congenital deformity** can occur due to genetic problems. Pregnancy is critical period. Foetal formation is adversely affected it the pregnant mother suffers German-measles, mumps, jaundice and other sense viral infections. Drug abuse among pregnant mothers may also result in the improper foetal formation of bones, limbs and other important body organs.

Causes of Social Disadvantage Amongst Children

Socially handicapped children find it different to have a place for themselves in the society, lack of social acceptance is due to the fact that they do not behave like the so called normal children of their age. They indulge in antisocial activities like stealy, pick-pocketing, gambling alchohol, drug abuse, and sexual behaviours, various causes leading to social handicap can be follow:

(a) **Broken Homes:** Children fall out from poor families where there is constant bickering among the parents. The children do not get the love and guidance due to them. They may even be deprived of the basic necessities of life and take to streets for survival unwanted children and orphan often fall victims of social maladjustments.

(b) **Poverty and Ignorance:** Children from very poor families and of ignorant parents are often deprived of food clothing, and shelter. In the absence of proper guidance from their parents, these children start petty thefts to survive. Later they get habituated to antisocial activities in a big way.

(c) **Inadequate Schooling:** School is the second place where the children learn the values of life. Poor parents do not send their children to school for want of funds. These children remain unguided in streets for long hours. They often get into gang fights and undesirable activities. Children also succumb to negative peer pressure when they do not have strong normal and social values from parents, teachers and other adults.

(d) **Lack of Good Models:** Children have very sensitive minds and learn fast from adults in their environment. Living with concept and dishonest persons give negative values to the children. They fail to differentiate between right and wrong. Moral values are not taught like they used to be in olden days. Children imbibe these values from adults and siblings at home, from teachers and peers at school. Problems arise when they have wrong individuals as their note models.

(e) **Lack of Supervision during the Formative years:** This can happen children from poor as well as rich families. Poor parents have to put in long hours of watch to sustain life while which ones overlook/neglect the upbringing their desire to become richer. These parents leave the upbringing of their children to the avoids and servants. Parents should be committed to the upbringing of their children, specially during the formative years.

Ways to Help Disadvantaged Children

The various ways of helping disadvantaged children are listed below:

(a) Lots of love and parental support is essential.

(b) Proper guidance by trained teachers/special educator/parents/siblings and peers.

(c) Individuals coming in contact with special child should be good role madels. Their enables the disadvantaged child to eliminate the ideal model and learn the task well.

(d) These children should have high level of motivation. They should be given lots of opportunities and encourgement to learn and perform. The extend of learning depends upon repetition and the effort taken to master the skill/lesson/task.

(e) The "differently abled" children require lot of patience and encouragement from family.

(f) Special exercises and therapies and techniques promote better learning.

(g) Handicapped children should be given special aids that will enable them to overcome their limitations.

(h) Interaction with peers is equally important peer group provides "identity" to the handicapped child.

(i) Adult and peers coming in contact with the disadvantaged child need to possess good human values and considerations.

(j) These coming in contact with special children should not snigger at their awkwardness.

(k) Government and voluntary agencies should provide these children with the basic needs of life. It takes a lot of time and effort to get these children on the right track.

(l) Socially disadvantaged children need special attention for education, skills and behavioural modifications for rehabilitation in the society.

(m) Lastly no effort should be spared to make these children self reliant, happy, physically and emotionally strong for the family and society to be proud of.

Bibliography

Baldwin, A.L. (1955), Behaviour and Development in Childhood, New York.

Bayley, N. (1975), On the Growth of Intelligence, American psychologist.

Bereiter C. and Engleman S. (1966), Teaching Disadvantage Children in the Pre-school.

Bowlby, J. (1951), Maternal Care and Child Health.

Hurlock, E. (1972), Child Development. Tokyo.

Kohlberg, L. (1964), Development of Moral Character and Moral Ideology, New York.

Kohlberg, L . (1968), Early Education, a Cognitive Development View, Child Development.

Kohlberg, L. (1974), Moral Development and Faith.

Lenneberg, E.H. (1967), Biological Function of Language.

Panda, K.C. (1978), Elements of Child Development.

Piaget, J. (1932), The Moral Judgment of the Child, London.

Piaget, J. (1952), The Origins of Intelligence in Children, New York.

Piaget, J. (1968), Six Psychological Study, London.

Index

A

B

C

D

E

F

K

L

M

N